"In an effort to promote good and safe work practices…"

YOU AND YOUR NEW HOME

Protecting Yourself
From Common Mistakes

JEFF CROSS

Published by:
J Cross Books
jcrossbooks.com

ISBN 978-0-9825793-0-5

The information contained in this book is from the unique perspective of the author. The author does not warrant any of the information within and urges the reader to research any information obtained. This is not a "How to Build a House" book. This is more of a *how to recognize common mistakes* book. To keep the cost of this book down, it is kept as brief as possible. Common mistakes and oversights which the author has personally encountered are brought to your attention to help to prevent the same occurrences from affecting your project. Some of the designs may be regionally limited.

CONTENTS

INTRODUCTION

As a building inspector it is my job to protect consumers from the mistakes and oversights of building contractors as well as their subcontractors. The United States construction industry has moved from craftsmen learning a trade through an apprenticeship to entrepreneurs building "cookie cutter" homes utilizing unskilled laborers. It has become more important than ever to gain knowledge to protect yourself.

Custom homes are now built exactly like "spec homes" and the same mistakes are made repeatedly. Spec homes are homes which are repeated over and over within a neighborhood. Many homeowners now hire real estate inspectors or construction consultants to perform inspections during construction. If this option is available to you, then use it. There is no comparison to having a trained set of eyes watching over a project which you'll be paying on for thirty years or more.

Master craftsmen are few and far between. When you find one, you've accomplished something! Looking at work your builder has done in the past was typically a good way to judge the type of work they would do. All builders, though, are in business to make money. So, in turn is the challenge:

A builder will hire subcontractors to build their homes. For example, a dirt contractor will go out and prepare the site. When he has completed this portion of the job, he receives his pay and goes to the next one. Now, his dozer breaks down and it costs him $9,000 to repair it. Therefore, he goes to the builder and says he is going up on his prices to offset the cost of his equipment repair. The builder has quoted your house already and the extra cost is not allotted in his bid, so he calls someone else to do the site work at your house.

The builder may implement at any time during the construction process. What you look at may have been constructed by an entirely different group of people. The builder basically just coordinated everything. Now I am not discounting the importance of coordination, because without it, the work will not come together. Moreover, the builder does more than coordination and a good builder who is vigilant has all my respect.

The fact is, no matter what the evidence, things change and you need to know what to watch for. In this book, we'll cover aspects of many basic building practices. I will introduce you to the International Residential Code (IRC), and I am hopeful you will be a comfortable with what you observe as you visit your new home site each day.

Please let me introduce myself. I am Jeff Cross and a building inspector in a medium to small city in Texas. At the time this edition was written, our city had adopted the 2003 International Building Codes. The State of Texas does not require builders to obtain a license and basically, anyone can be a builder. Any construction outside the city needs no inspections.

I've been in construction all my life, owning my first construction company while I was still in my teens. In high school, I would assist my father in pouring concrete flat work and constructing steel buildings. Eventually I went into the plumbing business, as my father was a master plumber. I then moved into mechanical work (A/C and heating), and then into electrical work.

At this time, I hold certifications for building, plumbing, mechanical, energy conservation, and electrical inspections through the International Code Council (ICC). I also hold several other license and certifications for commercial inspections which do not apply here.

I firmly believe you are better protected in a city or a jurisdiction where building inspections are performed. Even where inspections occur, you are vulnerable to oversights. Keep in mind this very important fact: the building code is the worst the building should be. If the structure is to code, it doesn't say much; just that it is safe for occupancy. A building inspector is limited in what he/she can enforce by the model code which has been adopted. A builder is capable of exceeding the requirements of the code and you must demand this.

If you would like to obtain a copy of a building code go to International Code Council's web site at *www.iccsafe.org*, or speak to the building official within your jurisdiction to find which code they have adopted. Most building inspectors will try to answer questions if they can.

These are the basic items we'll talk about:

- Site work and utilities
- Plumbing ground work
- Foundation
- Framing
- Electrical rough-in
- Plumbing top-out
- Mechanical rough-in (duct)
- Drywall and fire protection
- Final inspections
- Energy Conservation

I will not cover the following items in this book:

- Your contract between you and your builder – This is a legal issue and should be treated as such.
- Any permitting information

- Designing your home – There are minimum requirements for designing homes which are so small it is difficult to mess this up. You need to be happy with your lay out, if you need help with this, an architect would be a better source than me.
- Choosing your lot – I have a couple of tips in the section about site work. Other than that, well, there are too many things to cover. An architect may help you here if you need it. I think you probably have your place already if you have bought this book.
- Basements – This subject would take an entire book by itself. There are a lot of books out there covering basements.
- Swimming Pools
- Decks and Porches
- Cabinets and trim – These are not structural and vary to an infinite degree.

SITE WORK
AND UTILITIES

WOODED LOTS

If you have a wooded lot, you most likely will not be able to save all the trees. Meet with your builder after you have chosen where to place your home on the site and stake the general location if you can. Some locations have too much vegetation to get through. This means a weekend of fighting poison ivy and wasps.

Staking out the house will give you an idea where the trees will be in relation to your home. You don't want a tree closer than about ten feet from the foundation since roots will be cut, and you may be removing it in the future when the injury has caused it to die. Roots may affect the foundation. Debris from the trees may also affect any gutter systems, patios, balconies or inside corners. Don't forget in some areas, pests are a consideration when dealing with trees close to the house.

SLOPE

Any slope in excess of 2% will usually ring some bells for your builder. A good lot is considered to be less than a 2% slope. What he means is $\frac{1}{8}$ inch per 12 inches of fall or more exists. This doesn't sound like much, does it? Think of it this way; if you have a structure fifty feet long, and the slope drops 1/8 inch per foot, then you'll drop fifty eighths, or 6 1/4 inches.

1

The garage will be here.

Pad is raised to allow accessible driveway.

For the builder, this means either filling in or cutting down. For you, this means more money. Dirt work is expensive and in some areas it is limited by climate. If the decision to cut is made, and if the soil type will allow it, soil will be moved from the high side to the low side. This is the best-case scenario. Top soil is made up of soil which still has decomposition occurring or silt and other types of unstable materials.

If the decision is made to bring in fill dirt, then you want to make sure it is of a quality which will make a stable pad. If it is possible to be on site when the soil is delivered, watch for the following: roots, debris, ashes or burned soil or uneven mixtures of soil types such as chunks of clay in gravel fill. Also watch for expansive soils, which are soils that hold a lot of water and shrink when they dry out.

PAD

The pad is basically what your house is going to sit on. It extends from undisturbed soil to the bottom of the concrete slab or where the skirting starts on a pier and beam house. Undisturbed soil is typically 12 inches below grade.

Fill

When the fill dirt is spread, it should be spread out in six to eight inch layers. Each layer is called a "lift" and each lift must be compacted. This can be accomplished by driving a loaded dump truck or water truck back and forth until the tires have pressed it down uniformly. A tracked dozer will NOT "do it as good." The tracks on tracked equipment are designed to spread the weight out and the compaction will not reach its full potential.

This pad was built up 12 feet. (24 "lifts")

The elevation of the lot must be considered as well. This will affect your utilities as well as how you enter and exit. The driveway must be usable, so don't skimp on fill just to require four wheel drive to get out of the garage. 12 1/2% is a typical slope for a driveway. This is a 2 inch fall per foot. Mowing is a concern when building a pad in a high slope area. We'll address the utilities in below.

Keep in mind your pad must direct rain water away from the house and in the direction it would have traveled before you began building. The exception would be where the water is required to go out to the gutter by the authority having jurisdiction.

If you are building in or near a flood plain, you definitely want to keep this in mind when determining the elevation of your pad.

SITE UTILITIES

The builder may, and should watch for the following. If he doesn't, it can be costly.

SEWER

The first utility normally addressed is the sewer. If a public sewer system is available then half of the battle is won. You want to verify the elevation of the sewer main so the drain system will drain by gravity. This should be checked before your site preparation begins, seeing as it will directly affect the elevation of the house. I personally dealt with a builder who cut down a lot 4 feet only to find the sewer main was only 2 feet deep. The builder was forced to install an expensive pumping system to dispose of waste.

If public sewer is not available then an On Site Sewage Facility (OSSF) must be utilized. Different places handle OSSF's in various ways. In Texas, they are controlled by the State via a designated representative for each county and municipality. Look in to this before you begin because the cost can be enormous. Different soil types will affect the design and, the size of your lot can even make it unbuildable.

POWER

Electrical power is also a must. If a power line runs over head, look for the transformer closest to you. That will most likely be where you'll get it from. If you are a quarter mile off the road, you may have to pay the power company to run a line to your home. Call the power company and ask them to send a consultant out to meet you on site. They usually do this free of charge.

GAS

Gas is a nice utility to have. Don't discount it before you read the chapter on efficiency. If gas is locally available, you'll want to have one of the service provider's consultants tell you where the lines are. It is difficult to run a new gas line under a driveway or around other structural and natural barriers. The plumber can stub out for gas where it is needed, instead of where it is convenient for him.

PLUMBING
UNDERGROUND

The plumbing underground is installed after the pad is completed, the rough forms are in place, and after any sub-grade footers are installed. The pad inside the forms should be flat and consist of sand or a soft non-expansive soil that can be spread out. Some areas will use a layer of gravel. The plumber will excavate the ditches for the drain lines placing pipe in the ditches using the soft soil or sand to bed the pipes in as he goes.

DRAIN

The most common drain system is made of schedule 40 PVC. The pipes will be marked for use in drain, waste and vent systems (DWV). A riser will extend up at each place a fixture or stack is to be placed. A stack is a vent or drain, which will go to the second floor. You may have a riser, which is 10 feet tall. This is a pressure test. All the risers are capped off except the tall one which is then filled with water. The weight exerts pressure on the system for leak detection. This is called a ten-foot head.

The entire system can be capped off and air pressure can be placed on the system. 5 psi would be the ideal amount as 5 psi is the same pressure that the 10 foot head is. The PVC cannot handle much more. Demand to see one of these tests.

1/10th pound increments will show any leaks within a 15 minute test.

The slope of the pipe is another thing to look for. Get an accurate four foot level and tape a 1/2 inch spacer to one end. When you place the level on the pipe, and it shows level, then an exact 1/8 inch per foot fall is being used. Make sure the spacer is on the end pointing toward the sewer main. Using a small level, such as a torpedo level is not accurate enough.

3 and 4 inch pipes should have a slope of 1/8 to 1/2 inch per foot. 2 1/2 to 1 1/2 inch pipes should run between 1/4 to 1/2 inch per foot.

PVC joints in the pipe must be cemented together using a primer that is purple in color and a solvent cement that is not purple. This is a code requirement. Without the primer, the manufactures listing is invalid. A clear "cleaner" is NOT a replacement for purple primer. The word cleaner and the word primer do not mean the same thing!

The next thing to watch for is dips in the piping system. Earlier I said the pipe must be bedded in. It is very important this occur to prevent dips in the pipe. The pipe is laid on a flat firm bed. Soft soil or sand is filled in on both sides of the pipe and tamped down tight around it. You should be able to see just enough of the pipe to determine its size and material. I walk down each piece and it should not move as I do (and I am a fat man!).

Concrete Chunks

Piece of brick

This bedding is not compacted

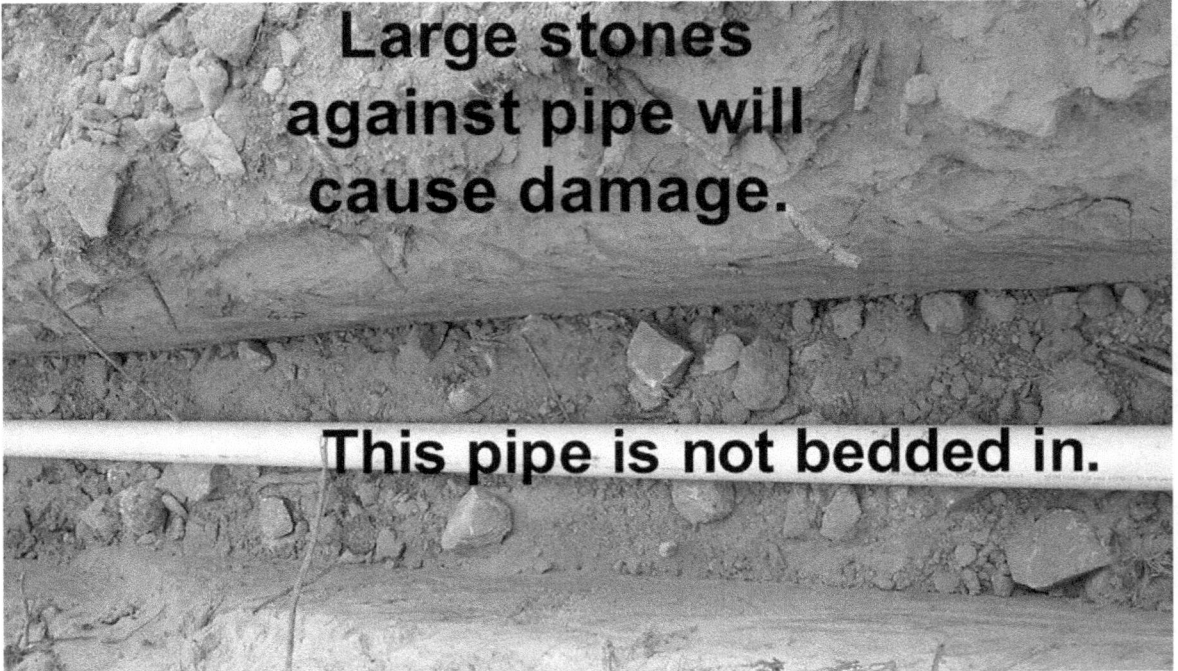
Large stones against pipe will cause damage.

This pipe is not bedded in.

Well bedded pipes.

The ditch should be backfilled six inches and compacted so the concrete crew has less chance of damaging the pipe. When the concrete crews dig beams, the ditch where the piping is should not cave into the beam.

Double clean-out fitting within 5 feet of foundation.

The sewer is stubbed out on the side of the house pointing toward the sewer tap or OSSF. A clean out fitting is placed within 5 foot of the house at this point.

On pier and beam homes, the drain isn't placed in ditches under the house. They should be supported off of the ground from the floor framing above. The pressure test is performed later in the top-out stage. The transition from the building drain system to the sewer is typically be made at the edge of the house. The drop would be made at an angle so that stress will not be placed in other parts of the system when the house moves.

Take a look at the spacing of hangers used to support the drain and verify they do not exceed 4 feet on PVC pipes. The slopes must be maintained as described above.

Sizing of the drain system must be on a per house design. In the ground, you should not have a drain size smaller than 2 inches though code allows it. It is difficult to clean a stoppage in a line smaller than 2 inches due to the design of equipment used for the purpose. Additionally, examine your clothes washing machine drain. It will be 2 inch and should have no other fixture connected to it until it goes into a 3 inch or larger pipe.

The use of proper fittings is a very in depth study. These are things licensed personnel must know and use. It is imperative to check a workers license. Demand the worker on site is minimally licensed as a journeyman plumber. Some states and jurisdictions will allow a tradesman to plumb houses with less experience than a journeyman. If the master plumber comes to the site and checks each phase of work personally, chances are the work will be right or corrected if needed. Look at both of their plumbing license! If you want to know exactly what the plumbing license looks like, contact the authority having jurisdiction.

WATER

The water system may or may not be installed in this phase of the job. In warmer climates water may be run in the attic and inspected during the top-out phase. In cooler climates, the water is placed under the slab, brought together inside walls, and connected together in manifolds.

PEX manifolds

The material may be of copper or crosslinked polyethylene (PEX). Copper, being more expensive, is losing popularity while PEX has overwhelmed many markets. In some cases a single manifold is used and left accessible to the homeowner and individual lines are run to each fixture from this manifold.

Make sure copper lines are sleeved through concrete as the acidic nature of concrete will rapidly deteriorate the copper. PEX must be sleeved in areas being sprayed with pesticides because studies have shown pesticide carriers may pass through the material causing water to have a bad taste.

Either type of system must be tested before concrete is poured. The water distribution system can be tested with 50 psi of air or water. I've seen entire rolls of copper split on a test such as this. If it had not been tested, the lines under the slab would have been useless. PEX is susceptible to ultraviolet light. Piping stored outside may become damaged. This test most likely will help find piping damaged in this way.

Do not use PVC, CPVC or any other material which requires having joints under slabs. A "silver solder joint" on a copper pipe under a slab is not acceptable.

Bringing the water into the house in the slab is clean in appearance and should be done in this phase, though it isn't required in warmer climates.

FOUNDATION

Everything depends on the foundation. If it moves, the devastation can be serious. There are several types of foundations. Some are engineered and some aren't. The most common is known as slab on grade. Pier and beam is typically the least expensive. Since the most common is slab on grade, we'll cover it primarily but I will touch on the others too.

FOOTINGS

There should be no roots, grass or other materials which will decompose over time under your home. The footings of your foundation must extend 12 inches, minimum, into undisturbed soil. In some cases footings must extend further to get to a soil suitable for stability and to be below the frost line. If you can afford it, hire a geo-tech company to bore your site for the best information. The geo-tech's engineer will be able to recommend a proper depth when the soil is questionable. Residential builders will only do this if the authority having jurisdiction requires it, due to the cost. Call a local reputable foundation repair company if you are unable to use a geo-technical service, as they will be familiar with the area and may recommend a depth if needed.

This was the original elevaton.

These lots were shaved off for construction. All vegetation was removed and pads will be placed on the undisturbed soil.

PIERS

Some footings are simply bored piers. This is accomplished by a sub contractor boring holes under the points in the slab where load bearing beams will intersect and between those points where the span of the beam requires it. The driller will bore down to a soil type which appears stable. Some builders will have the driller bell the bottom of the pier to give it a larger bearing surface.

This pier will support the concrete beam. It extends down through the pad into undisturbed soil

Bored piers should not be left over night. They should be dry if possible, but should have no more than a couple inches of water if unavoidable. They can be pumped if water begins to enter. Loose soil must never be pushed back in the hole before the concrete is poured. That would place your footing on non-compacted soil, a big no no! The concrete is typically poured to the point where the bottom of the beam will be located.

16

SPREAD FOOTINGS

Spread, or block footings, are usually excavated rectangular holes. They would be strategically placed just as the piers are described above. The bottoms of the footings are firm and will not normally be very deep. They too will be a minimum of 12 inches into undisturbed or compacted soil. They are also used where bored holes will not work due to a high water table.

BEAMS

Beams are the most common footers used. They are the same beams which would sit on the footers above, but on a level lot or on a well compacted pad the footers may not be used. The beam would be at least 12 inches wide and 12 inches deep measuring from the top of grade for a single story home. Grade would be where the concrete floor would come into contact with the pad.

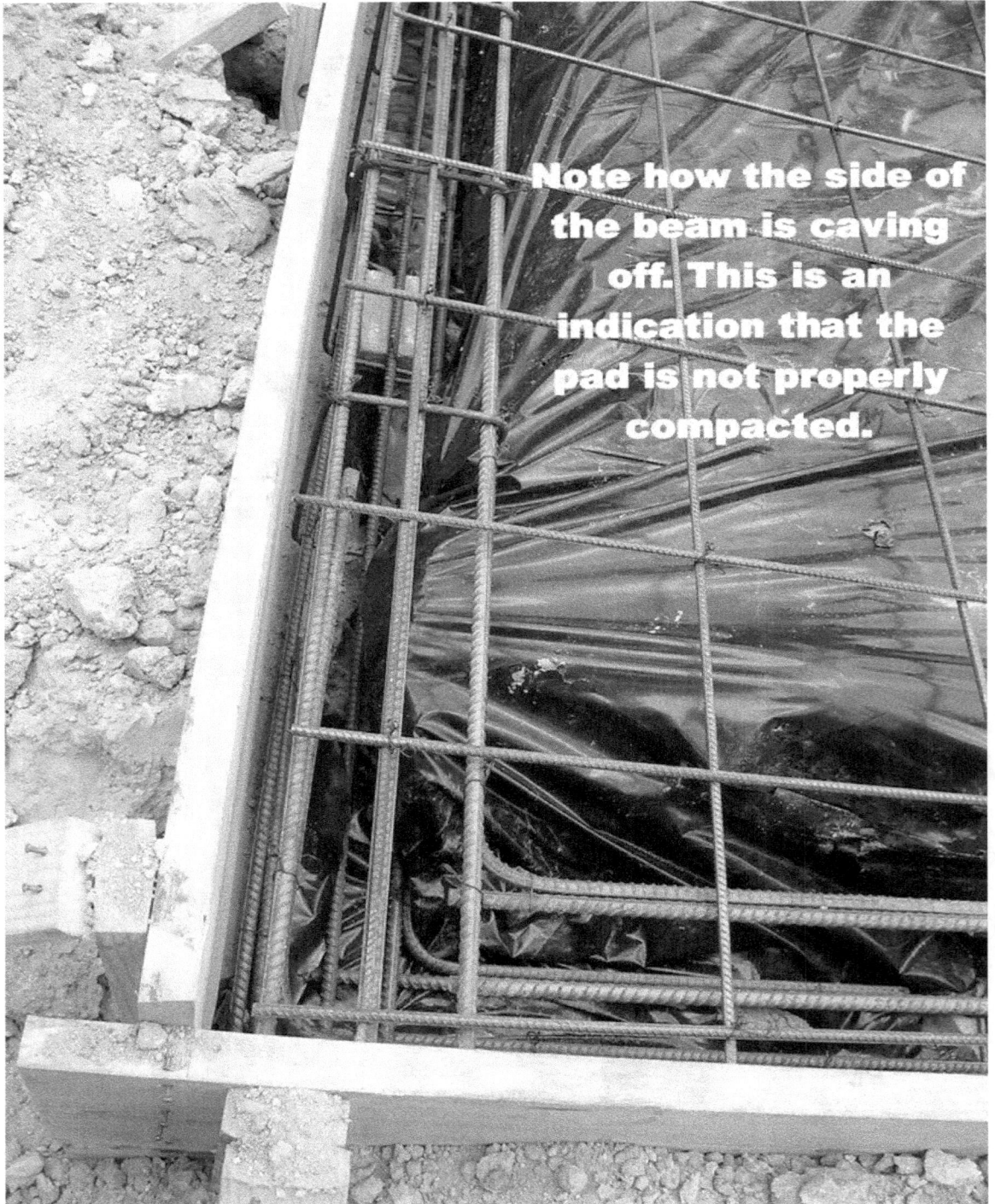

Note how the side of the beam is caving off. This is an indication that the pad is not properly compacted.

RE-BAR

Footers and beams are usually built with reinforcing steel in the concrete. Concrete will break with or without steel in it. The reinforcing steel is what will hold it together when it does break. The beams spanning footers or directly on grade must maintain its strength even when the concrete breaks. Code requires a minimum of 2 reinforcing steel bars of 1/2 inch diameter in a beam. Personally I think more is better. It is not uncommon for a single story house to have 4 bars per beam. 2 placed 2 inches off the bottom, and 2 placed 2 inches below the floor. Most concrete contractors will tie the top bars at the same level as the bars placed in the 4 inch thick floor. The important thing is the re-bars be placed in a way to allow at least 2 inches of concrete to incase them.

When the contractor speaks about the size of re-bar, he will use numbers such as Number three or Number five. Don't let this rattle you. Re-bar is sized in 1/8 inch increments. A Number three bar is 3/8 inches in diameter. A Number five would be 5/8 inch in diameter.

SLAB ON GRADE

Your slab is basically the floor. It extends over the beams to the inside edge of the forms. The beams are normally poured monolithically with the floor. When you look at your foundation, the concrete subcontractor will be ready to pour. It is very important you slow things down just a little. This is a very critical inspection. Take your time and ask questions if you're not sure.

ENGINEERED SLAB

It is possible the authority having jurisdiction or conditions at the site will require you to have an engineered foundation. If your foundation is engineered, you need to have the most recent design with the engineers stamp and signature on it. You want to read ALL the notes on his design. If any item is not per his design, then he no longer holds responsibility. Therefore the installation must be per his design EXACTLY. If it isn't, then the engineer must approve any changes in writing. Do not allow the builder to pour concrete if the engineer is not 100% convinced that it's ready. The only way to prove inconsistencies is to tear it out. Photos may not always do it!

The engineer's notes will dictate every detail of the installation.

Live end of Tendon

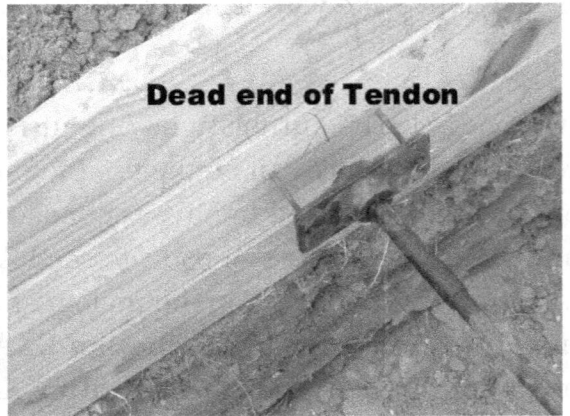

Dead end of Tendon

NON-ENGINEERED SLAB

If the slab on grade is not engineered, look for the following:

- No soil should be between the footers and the beam.
- The pad under the floor area must be firm, flat and have no dirt clods or soft spots. If you can push a Number 4 re-bar into the pad more than 4 inches, be concerned. The plastic may need to be pulled back to allow drying.
- A 6-mil vapor barrier must be in place covering the entire pad. In comparison a kitchen trash bag is only 0.9 to 1.2-mil.
- Reinforcing steel must be in place and supported 2 inches off the bottom or in the center of the floor. Stretch a string across the top of the form and measure between the tightly pulled string and the top of the pad. The steel should be in the middle.
- The minimum size of reinforcing in a poured on grade floor is nonexistent in the code. Personally, Number 3 re-bar on 16 inch centers each direction would be my minimum. More is better.
- A "concrete encased grounding electrode" must be installed in a beam. This item is forgotten a lot. Usually it will be installed near the electrical panel box, although it can be anywhere in a wall. Look for a Number 4 re-bar (or larger) sticking up in an outside wall. It will continue down into a beam and tie to, or run alongside one of the lower bars in the beam. Either way works. If it is tied, make sure it is tied in at least three places to the bottom bar. Under this bar, there should be no plastic vapor barrier for 20 feet. This is so the ground can conduct a fault to the earth. It is difficult for electricity to pass through the plastic barrier. Verify it is not in a door where it will have to be removed later.

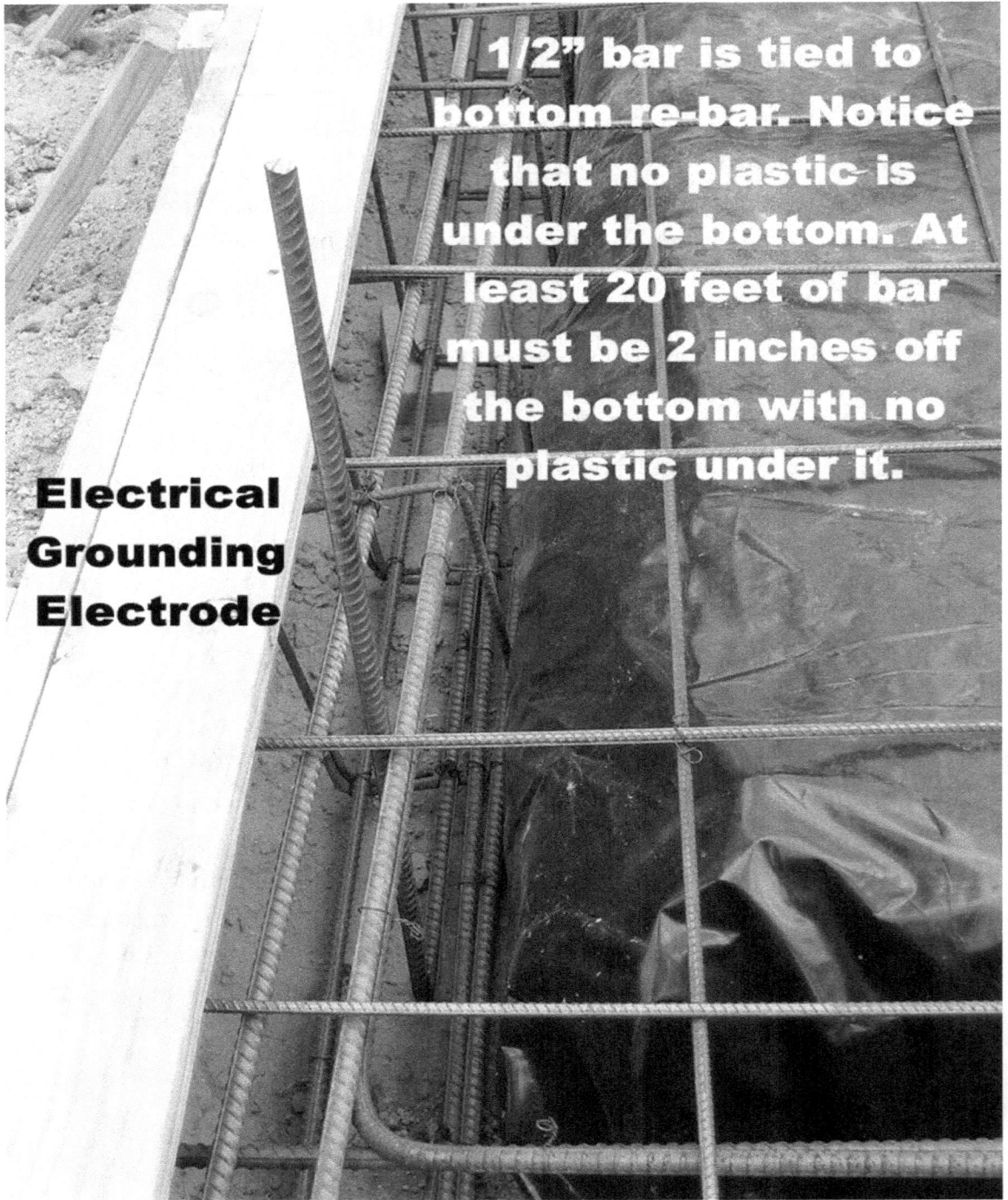

1/2" bar is tied to bottom re-bar. Notice that no plastic is under the bottom. At least 20 feet of bar must be 2 inches off the bottom with no plastic under it.

Electrical Grounding Electrode

At this time, the conduit must be installed for any islands you will have. An island in a kitchen must have at least one electrical outlet (unless it's moveable).

While looking at the beams, observe the plumbing pipes. When they pass through the beams, they should be sleeved through another piece of pipe two pipe sizes larger. This sleeve should extend into the pad on both sides of the beam. This will prevent concrete from entering the sleeve. Using sleeves allows the soil to move without damaging the pipe. Wrapping cardboard around the pipe instead of using a sleeve does not accomplish the same task. This applies to drains AND water pipes. If a riser comes into a beam and stubs up through the slab, then of course it can't be sleeved.

This pipe passes through the beam. It should be sleaved through a pipe two pipe sizes larger than itself.

In areas where termites are a problem, a pretreatment of the soil under the vapor barrier or other preventative measures may need to be addressed. Some opt to utilize a Bora-Care treatment which is applied to the framing rather than the soil. Contact a licensed pest control applicator for recommendations in your area.

Look for the anchor bolts. They should extend 7 inches into the concrete and be 1/2 inch diameter minimum. This means they will be need to be about 10 inches long. The extra length is to allow the bolt to pass through the sill plate.

WOOD FOUNDATIONS

A lot of designs are out there, and most of them work well. Many original designs are actually a combination of wood and masonry. It would be impossible to cover all of them, so let's look at certain important aspects. The basic design is; the piers set spaced throughout the house pad. The girder beams set on and are connected to the piers. Floor joists of 2X material (2X8, 2X10...) are set on edge on the girders. The subfloor will attach on the joists to complete the wood foundation.

Any wood within 18 inches of the ground should be pressure treated lumber, as well as heavy girders within 12 inches. Wood which comes into contact with concrete or stone should also be pressure treated. Any pier or column must be able to maintain its natural strength in any condition it is subject to encounter.

Girder/Beam — Sub-Floor — Floor Joist — Tie together — Column or pier

The footers, columns, girders and wall panels must be tied together to resist wind loads which push horizontally AND will create an uplift effect on the entire structure. Keep in mind some parts of the country have higher wind loads than others and seismic activity will also affect the entire structure. In these areas it is strongly recommended to ask the advice or use an engineer.

Watch for fasteners and their locations. Below grade, request stainless steel; above grade, exposed to elements galvanized steel must be used. Bolts used in foundation are typically 1/2 inch in diameter or larger. Lengths of nails will normally be one penny per eighth of an inch of board. A two inch board would use a 16d nail. However, this is not always the rule.

FRAMING

The frame of the house contains many very important components most people do not see. And many framing tasks are performed out of habit not knowing why! It is important that you understand why framing members are used in various method. This will help you help yourself.

The most important rule in framing is **all loads must be transferred directly through the framing members and foundation to the ground**. Any load imposed, including wind, snow and seismic, should be able to be traced all the way down.

We will look at the following things in this chapter:

- Wind loads (and seismic loads)
- Fire stopping and fire blocking
- Moisture penetration
- Chases
- Headers
- Spans

WIND LOADS

ENGINEERED FRAMING
Once again, when you deal with an engineered structure, read all the notes. Direct any questions to the person whose name is on the engineer's stamp. Engineers deal with all loading questions within a design. All prefabricated structural elements must be designed by an engineer. This includes trusses, I-joists or manufactured beams. Ask for a copy of the shop drawings and layouts when dealing with trusses. I am not an engineer and I ask the engineer about anything I don't FULLY understand. I implore you to do the same.

The most common mistake made in relation to trusses is other subcontractors drilling holes or cutting notches into engineered components. If any portion of a truss, I-joist or manufactured beam is altered in any way, verify if the engineering will allow it. If any one of the engineered components are altered in a non-allowable manner, then the engineer must design a repair or "fix" for the damaged component. A photo of a truss repair is in the "Trusses" section later in the book.

NON ENGINEERED FRAMING

When dealing with wind loads, either angle bracing corners, using plywood or oriented strand board (OSB) are the most common methods. Again, the wind speed has a direct affect on the design. Contact your local building official or refer to the International Residential Code for those specifications if needed.

Remember the strongest shape is a triangle. Wind bracing can be 1X4s set into the studs and plates at an angle, or a steel strap nailed to the studs and plates in an "X" configuration. The steel strap design is also used on ceilings, but these are normally on engineered designs.

Tying the framing members together using engineered steel straps are common in high wind areas as well as seismic areas. There are several brands to choose from but I am most familiar with Simpson. They have a nice web site at www.strongtie.com where you can get an online catalog. It is important to remember that ties are engineered and they specify specific fasteners to be used. Every nail hole will typically be used. If the "assembly" does not appear to fit properly, then it is probably wrong.

Joints in framing should be neat and tight. There should be no nails sticking out the side of a board. We call nails sticking through panels and not in framing members "shiners". When looking at a panel used for wind bracing, the nail pattern is important. Along each edge of the panel, you'll want the nails closer together. And in the field, the portion of the panel other than the edges where it attaches to intermediate supports would have a wider spacing for the nails. On walls, subfloors, and roof panels of 5/16 to 1/2 inch thick, I look for 6 inches on the edge and 12 inches in the field.

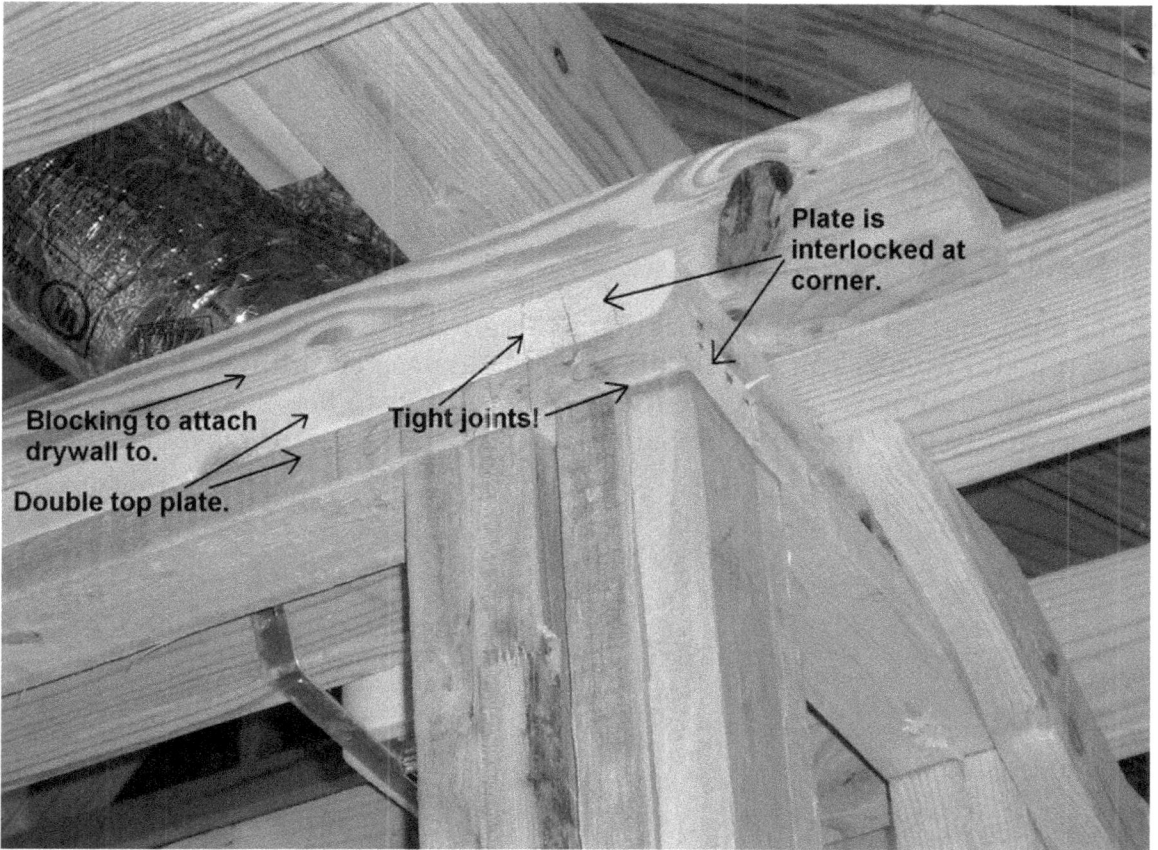

Plate is interlocked at corner.

Blocking to attach drywall to.

Tight joints!

Double top plate.

Most connections between two framing members are made with 2 or 3 nails. When the new guy gets his hands on the nail gun and starts popping 16 nails in a joint, it isn't because it will be stronger. In fact it is quite the opposite. If a framing member is split out from being gnawed on by a nail gunner, make him replace it on his own time... well, it needs to be replaced.

FIRE BLOCKING

Fire blocking is a simple concept that few framers of the "non-craftsman" variety understand. The concept is:

If a fire starts and burns through the wall covering, then slow the fire from FREELY moving to another part of the structure, especially areas that are concealed like chases, crawlspaces and attics. Look at a framed wall where a nine-foot ceiling is on one side and an eight-foot ceiling is on the other. If a fire starts on one side of the wall and burns through the drywall, once it's inside the wall, does it have a clear path above the lower ceiling? Materials commonly used for fire blocking are:

- 2X lumber
- 1/2 inch sheetrock
- 23/32 Plywood or OSB

Make sure that all of the fire blocking is installed tightly and seams are overlapped. Fire blocking should be found in changes of ceiling height, chases, fabricated columns, arches, transitions from ceilings to floors above, any wall in excess of 10 feet, and in floor ceiling assemblies to prevent movement horizontally.

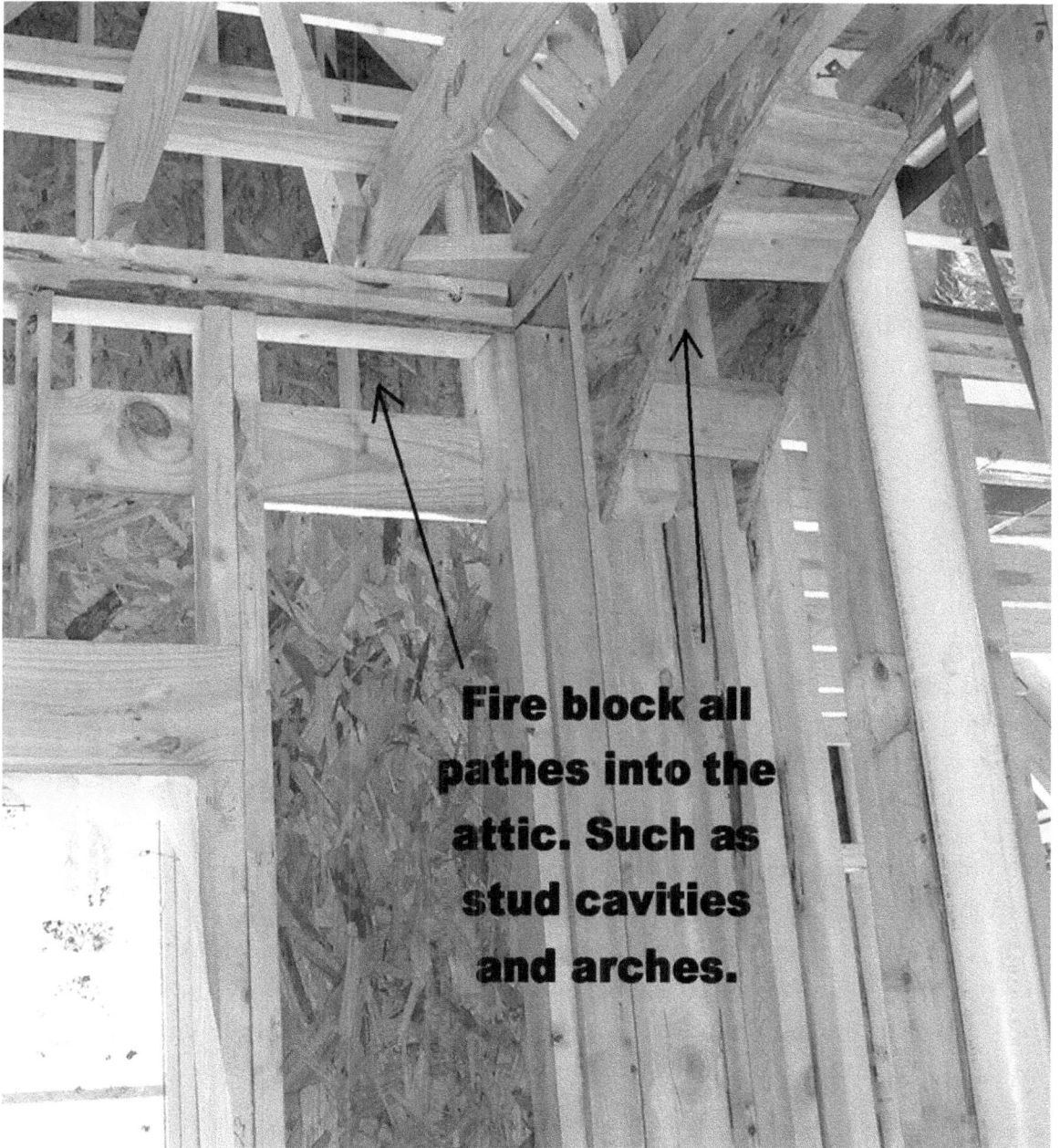

Fire block all pathes into the attic. Such as stud cavities and arches.

WALL FRAMING

The wall framing consists mainly of the following:

- Subfloor (Except slab on grade)
- Bottom plate (sill plate)
- Studs and corner posts
- Top plate
- Wall sheathing
- Headers on doors and windows
- Jack studs or trimmers

Since we are concerned about quality of workmanship, I will try to explain what components are and point out things to watch for as I go.

SUBFLOOR

The subfloor is the solid decking used to span the floor joists. It should extend to the outside edge of the girders. The subfloor panels must run perpendicular to the floor joists. Structural panels used for subfloors are of a type grade stamped with Doc PS-1, or Doc PS-2. A subfloor is always required when the floor joist are more than 16 inches apart.

BOTTOM PLATE

The bottom plate, sometimes called a sill plate or sole plate, will rest on the subfloor. On a concrete floor, the bottom plate is bolted to the floor with the 1/2 inch diameter anchor bolts we discussed in the section about foundations. It will be of a pressure treated 2X material. (2X4, 2X6 ...) Verify that anchor bolts are placed on exterior walls at least every 6 feet. They should also be within 12 inches of a splice in the plate, from a corner, and from a door.

STUDS

Studs should be straight and level. The minimum grade of a stud should be stud grade. In some cases, the code allows #3 and utility grade, but I recommend trying to improve on this. No stud should ever be longer the 10 feet and not be laterally supported.

TOP PLATE

The top plate of bearing walls will be two boards. Look for the splices in the plate; they should be staggered by at least 24 inches. At all intersecting walls and corners the plates should interlock. This is important as it adds strength to the entire structure when done properly.

These splices should be at least 24 inches apart. This spot creates a weak spot in the walls structure.

SHEATHING

Sheathing is the 4 foot by 8 or 10 foot plywood, OSB, or gypsum product used to cover the framing. Wall sheathing not only braces the wall vertically, but ties it all together. Since the panel is nailed to the bottom plate as well as the studs and top plate, the entire frame becomes a panel working as a unit. When wind loads strike the side of the home and try to lift the house upward the structure can transfer the negative load directly to the foundation. The bottom plate is fastened to the foundation with the anchor bolt and the sheathing panel prevents the studs from separating from the plates. Thus, we can trace the loads, negative or positive, to the ground. Some engineered designs use metal ties to tie the plates to the stud, and the sheathing may be a foam product for insulation rather than strength.

HEADERS

Headers are the horizontal members placed over openings in walls which are designed to support the structure above which the wall studs would support if there were no opening. The sizes of headers are determined by the load imposed on them and the span in which they reach. Inspectors utilize tables to calculate if headers and girders are of a size compliant with the tests performed by the grade mark testing agencies.

JACK STUDS & TRIMMERS

Jack studs, or trimmers, are the studs placed under the headers to support the weight and conduct it to the foundation. We don't want the weight supported by nails. If the span is more the about 9 feet on a one story, or 7 feet on a two story, look for 2 trimmers on each end of the header. Those are averages without seismic loading.

ROOF FRAMING

All wind loads on roofs react in several directions at once. So it is important to take your time and trace all the loads down. Snow loads affect the size of the framing members along with the general design and shape. Keep these in mind as you look everything over.

TRUSSES

Trusses are pre-manufactured framing components. Trusses can be used to support floors or roofs, and even walls are sometimes built as components. They are shipped to your site, unloaded, and stacked then lifted in to place on top of the walls like Tinker Toys. Each truss is composed of a top cord, a bottom cord and the webs running diagonally between the two. The joints are made with hydraulically applied connectors.

Bottom Cord Repair
Web
Connector

The trusses must be taken off the truck and placed onto a flat surface and stacked neatly. Not completing this simple task will destroy them over night. When they are being lifted, the manufacturer has lift points intended to be used. Look for the documentation on this. However, some will be marked on the truss itself.

After the components are installed, verify placement and orientation of every component. There is nothing like a floor with all the trusses upside down! Inspect every connector to see that none are missing or pulled loose. Look for any splits, cracks, or breaks in the boards. Any repair must be designed and documented on paper by the engineer of record. Check your documentation for any additional hardware, blocking or bracing which the engineer may require.

FRAMED ROOF

Simply put, the framed roof consists of ceiling joist which span each room for the ceiling to attach to. Rafters span from exterior walls to the center peak. The ridge board at the peak must be one board size larger than the rafters that lean into it. Bracing and girders add support to the rafters and direct the loads from the roof to the walls below.

As the roof framing presses down with the strength of gravity and snow or wind loads, the rafters tend to push the walls out making the house want to flatten out. The ceiling joists running in the same direction as the rafters, tie the ends of the rafters together preventing this action. If the joists run perpendicular to the rafters, then rafter ties are used to hold this pressure. They must connect to the rafters in the lower 1/3 of the peak height and connect to the corresponding rafter on the other side. Placement should be no more than 10 feet apart.

Where the rafters meet on a ridge board, they should align with the rafter on the corresponding side. Ridges and valleys, as well as any other bracing, must extend down to a wall or a beam. Bracing should never rest solely on the ceiling joists. Valleys should have a 2X running the length supporting it, and bracing from this 2X should run to walls capable of bearing the load.

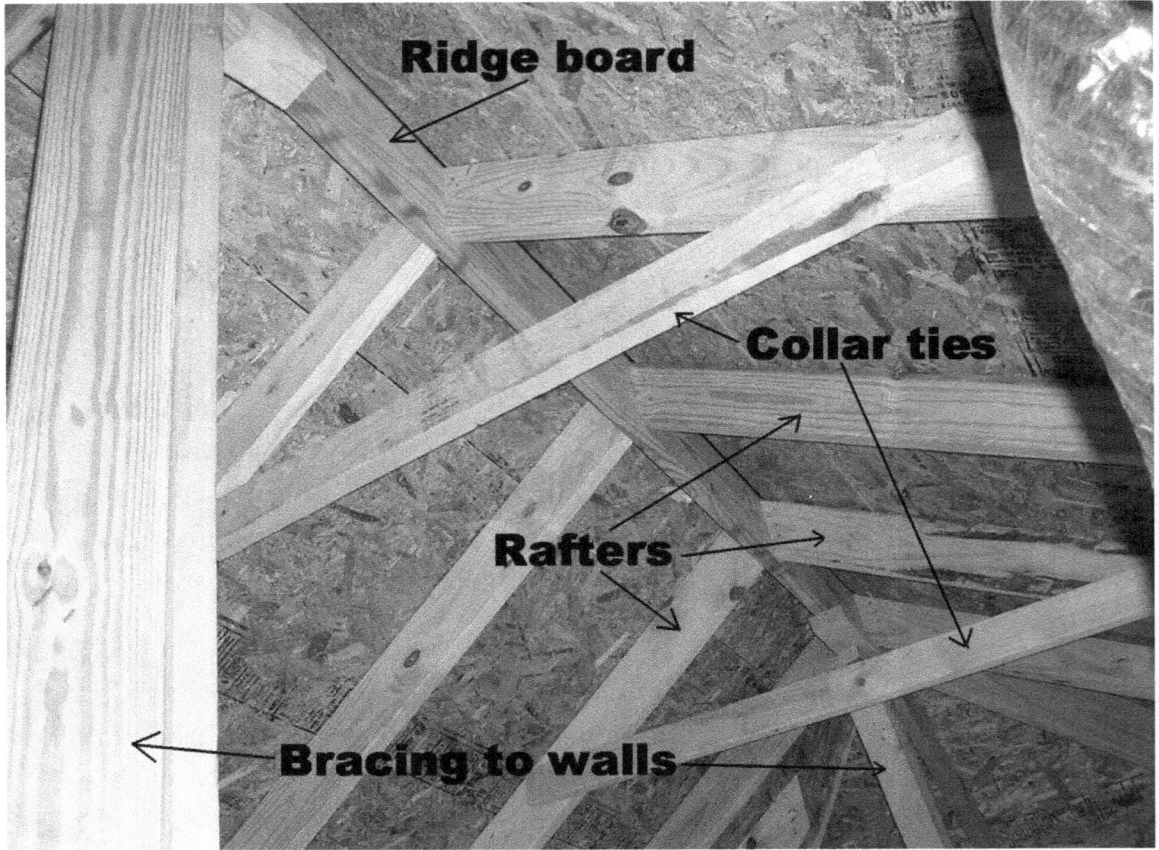

Ridge board

Collar ties

Rafters

Bracing to walls

MOISTURE BARRIERS

In my opinion, this particular subject is the most misunderstood part of residential construction. First, there are large differences between how moisture is dealt with in different regions. Where I am from, it's hot with 90% humidity ten months out of the year. Therefore, I am going to touch on the items which would be similar in most of the country, and point you toward other resources to deal with climates I know less about.

When you speak to your builder about a moisture barrier, some will only think of the material on the walls which prevent the migration of moisture through the walls. The fact is a barrier exists on all walls, the floor, and the roof. We covered the barrier in the floor in poured on grade concrete floors, but the pier and beam construction with a crawl space beneath the house must have a barrier as well. It may be similar to the type installed in the walls.

HOUSE WRAP

The walls would have a barrier such as tar paper or a material made specifically for the purpose. Tyvek is a brand most are familiar with. If the material is installed properly, then all the brands I've encountered work well. The key is proper installation.

Keep in mind materials used in construction are typically tested and graded to insure the product is compliant with the standards referred to in building codes. Each of the listings on the material requires it to be installed in a specific way in order for it to maintain its listing. 9 out of 10 installers have never seen the installation instructions, much less read them. If the builder is going to use Tyvek, then go to the website and get a copy of the installation instructions.
(*www2.dupont.com/Tyvek_Weatherization/en_US/tech_info/install*). If the builder is going to use another brand, go to their website and get the installation instructions.

If it is noted on your contract all materials used shall be installed per the manufacturers recommended installation methods, then the installer must comply.

This vapor barrier was not installed per the manufacturers recomended installation method.

FLASHING

Flashing is another part of the barrier which many builders lack an understanding. Flashing should be installed at the tops of exterior windows and doors. The exception is self flashed windows. Unfortunately, the instruction sheets are not read on these either. Siding must overlap these "U-shaped" frames by 1 1/8 inch. I've seen the siding applicators install the siding before the windows were even on the job! The only thing preventing a leak was a bead of caulk at the top of the trim.

Flashing should also be installed at any intersection of roof and wall, or any place where water can enter the structural portion of a wall or roof. A special note should be taken regarding chimneys or other structural elements which catch water. Verify a cricket is installed to divert rain around the piece. A "cricket", or saddle, is a ridge in the roof on the high side of a structural element where the ridge, running level, abuts the element and forces the water to go around the element instead of hitting the side full force. This is required by code on structures of thirty inches in width or more.

ELECTRICAL
ROUGH-IN

Copper or Aluminum? I thought this was answered in the 70's. Go with copper wire! I couldn't believe I was even asked this question.

As with most all the products out there, look for the UL label. If electrical parts or equipment doesn't have the UL label, don't allow the product to be used. I've found cable which looked exactly like other cable which was not listed with a label. The manufactures claim it's the same product and they don't have to pay for the listing label fee if it's not on there. This makes it more affordable, they say. I say, when an insurance inspector looks at the materials in a burned home and finds non-listed materials were used in its construction, it would be to your advantage to insist on listed materials. All building codes require it as well.

Here are the most common shortcomings I encounter in electrical installations:

WORKMANSHIP

When I see cables strung through an attic at odd angles, pulled tight around framing and twisted as if it was pulled out of the center of a coil, I think the electrician is more interested in saving money on material and time than protecting the lives put at risk by his installation methods. Cables should be placed in line with and attached to framing members and they should lay flat against them neatly.

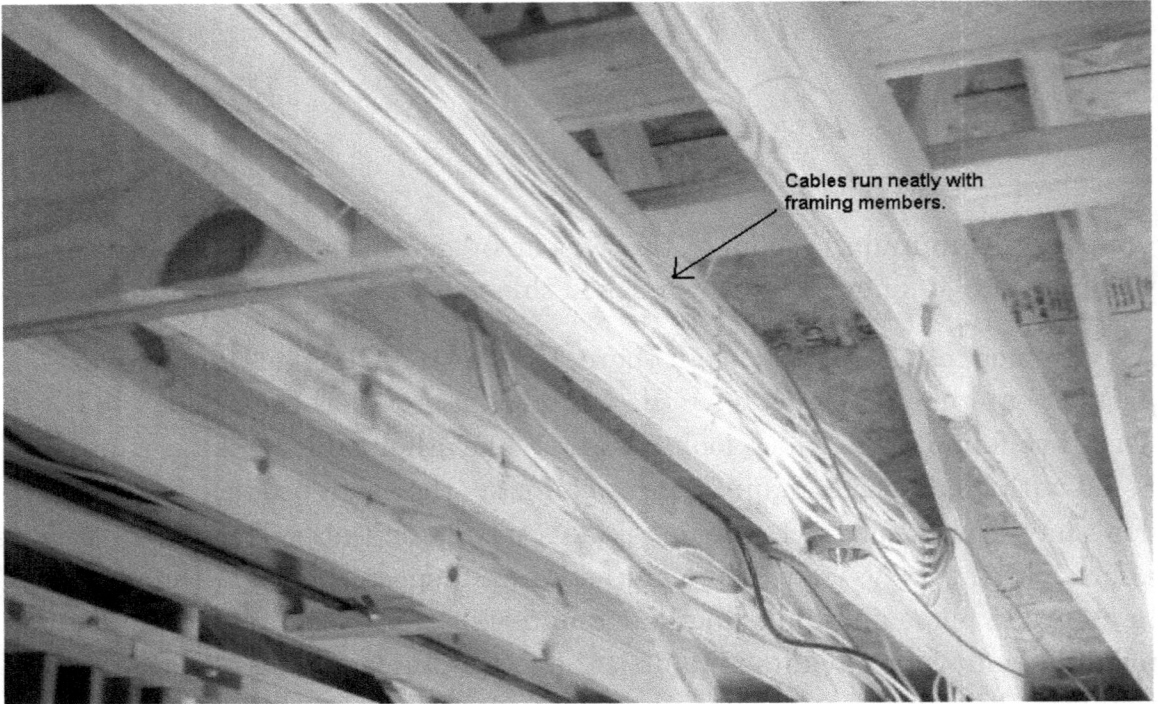

Cables run neatly with framing members.

Cables should terminate inside boxes with the cable's protective coating at least a half inch inside the box. A box prevents arcing or sparks from entering the wall cavity and starting fires. If a fault occurs, the wire insulation may become damaged, so you want the extra exterior coating inside the box.

These cables should extend into the box.

BENDING RADIUS

The bending radius must be five times the diameter of the cable. A normal circuit run in #12 would be about 5/8 of an inch wide. Use that dimension and watch for a radius about the size of a soda can when the cables make a turn.

NAIL PROTECTION

When cables pass through studs or other framing members, verify the surface the drywall is going to be attached to, is at least 1 1/4 inches from the cable. If it isn't, the contractor should install nail protection to prevent a sheetrock nail from damaging the cable. Also check for any damage to the cables where other subcontractors may be at fault.

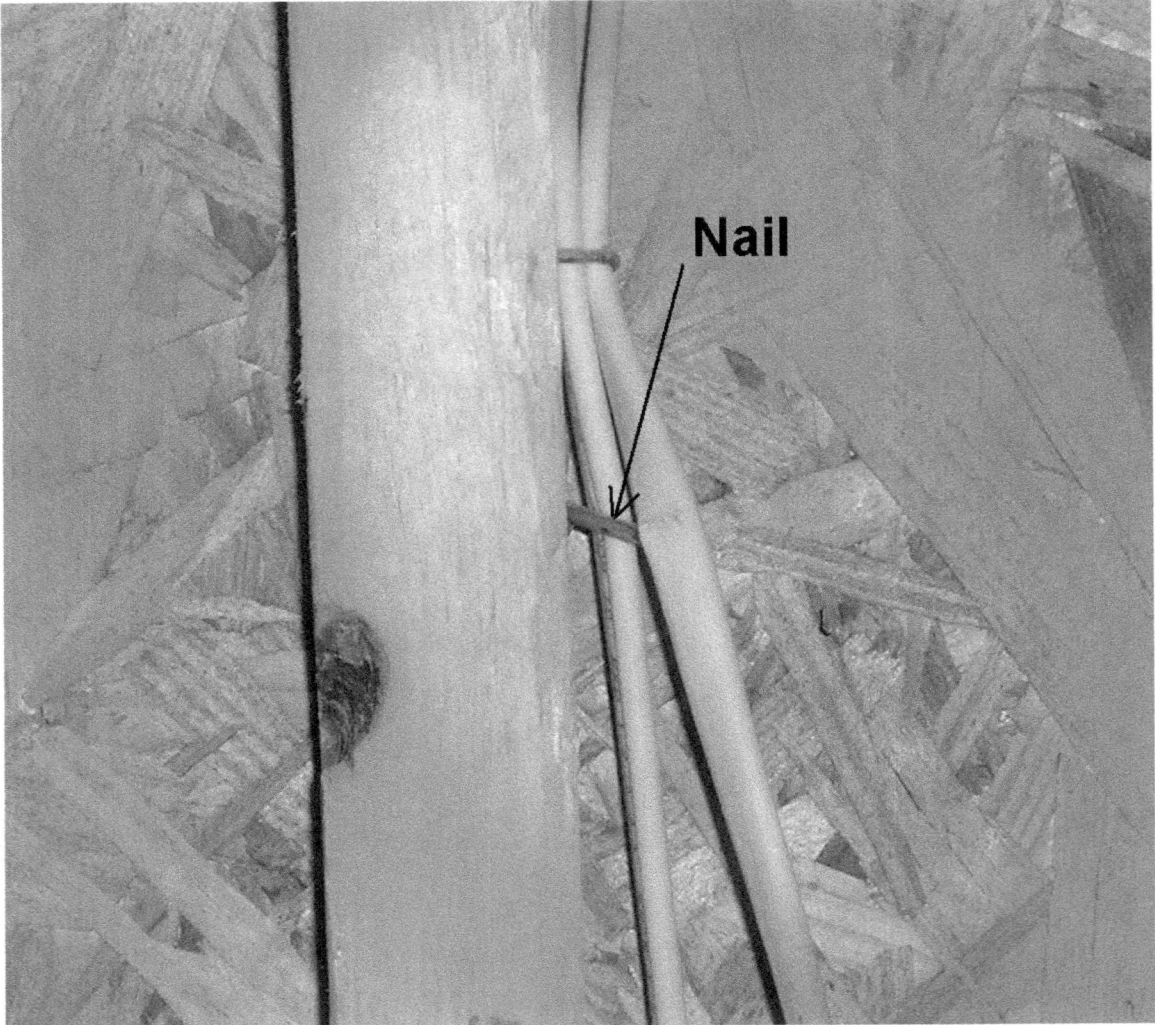

Nail

This cable was damaged by the framer who cut the stud to straighten it. Closely inspect all the cables and have damaged cables replaced, NOT REPAIRED.

Saw cut in stud.

GROUNDING

The grounding conductors are the most important wires in the electrical system. Verify a ground wire is connected to the concrete encased grounding electrode which was installed during the foundation installation. Other grounding must be connected as well, such as metal water pipes and ground rods near the main service.

SUB-PANELS

If other breaker panels are installed, called sub-panels, then verify there are four wires feeding it. The sub-panel will have a ground bar with green and bare wires attached to it. It will have a separate neutral bar which is insulated from the box with white wires connected to it. Then, it will have the phase conductors, which are the two big wires going to the main breaker in the panel.

Watch for interconnection between the two bars or a green screw in the neutral bar bonding it to the enclosure. Neither one should be present on a sub-panel although one must be present in the main panel.

GENERAL

Don't ask the electrician to install sconces, ceiling fans, or a chandelier over your garden tub. Not only are you placing yourself at more risk than you know, but the real estate inspector will catch this code violation when the next owners are looking to buy.

Check with your local power company consultant if you have questions about the electrical service. (i.e. meter socket and connection to the utility).

The top out is the portion of the piping system which extends from the floor and out of the roof. I will include the drain and vent system, the water distribution system and the gas piping.

DRAIN AND VENT

GENERAL

As each drainpipe extends up through the bottom plate, verify the size of the pipe is less than the size of the board it passes through. A 3 inch vent is too large for a 2X4 which is 3 1/2 inches wide.

Watch for drains and vents which are not running in a downward slope of about 1/8 inch per foot. Everything drains toward the sewer, including the vents. On two story (or larger) homes, the drain from one floor to the next is called a stack. There should be a clean-out at the base of each stack. It is to your advantage for these to be on exterior walls to allow cleaning of this part of the drain system to be done outside the house.

VENTS

Vents are installed for your protection. I will try to make the concept understandable even though I still find plumbers who don't "get it".

The vent is in place to protect a P-trap. This trap is essentially the gate way to Hell. The trap holds water creating a seal which is air tight. If the seal is not in place, then everything in the sewers have an open door into your home.

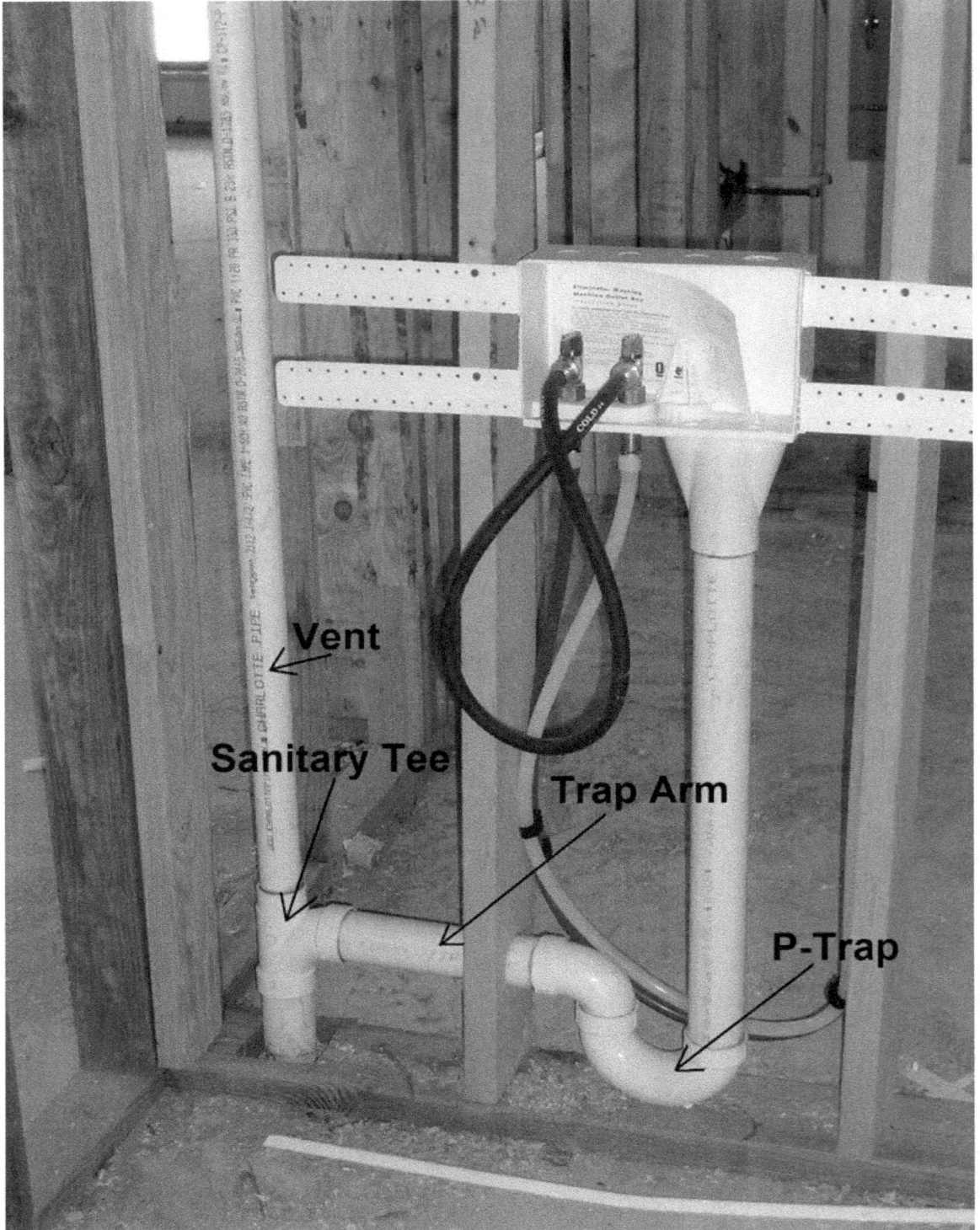

50

When the water is drained, the weight of the water in the sink pushes the water in the trap down the drain. As this plug of water descends, its weight pulls the water behind it as a siphon. When the basin is empty, the siphon will continue until it pulls the water in the trap out, leaving you unprotected. The vent, placed strategically up the line before the descent begins, breaks this siphon effect thereby keeping the gates of Hell closed.

The stub sticking out of the wall is the "trap arm". It almost always terminates into a fitting called a "sanitary tee". If one of the trap arms are in a fitting which looks different than the others, bring this up with the master plumber and have him explain how the trap will be protected.

A vent should extend high enough through the roof to prevent snow from blocking it. In some colder climates, the vent may be increased in size as it goes out to prevent frost from blocking it. Watch for support in the attics and under floors. 4 feet on PVC is the minimum on drains and vents.

TEST
The entire system should be pressure tested. Water can be placed on the entire system and leak tested. If water isn't available, air can be used up to 5 psi. It is harder to find leaks with air but if you observe the gauge is holding steady for 15 minutes then you'll know no leaks exist.

WATER SYSTEM

GENERAL
The smallest size of piping entering the house from the source should be 3/4 inch. The line entering and exiting from the water heater should be 3/4 inch as well.

 Placing the water heater(s) should be thought out when the building is designed. Hot water is best placed closest to appliances which use the most hot water. I disagree with water heaters being placed in attics. When they rupture and make a ceiling fall in with scalding water over a child's room the four square feet of marketable space no longer seems important. Watch the temperature and pressure (T&P) relief line. A 3/4 inch drain must be run for the T&P on the water heater. If it is run on the top-out phase, then watch for dips in the pipe. It must not be able to hold water at any point. It must be of 3/4 inch or larger copper, CPVC or PEX. It must not have a valve or a threaded end. I recommend they terminate outside, in a safe place pointing down and be close to the ground if possible.

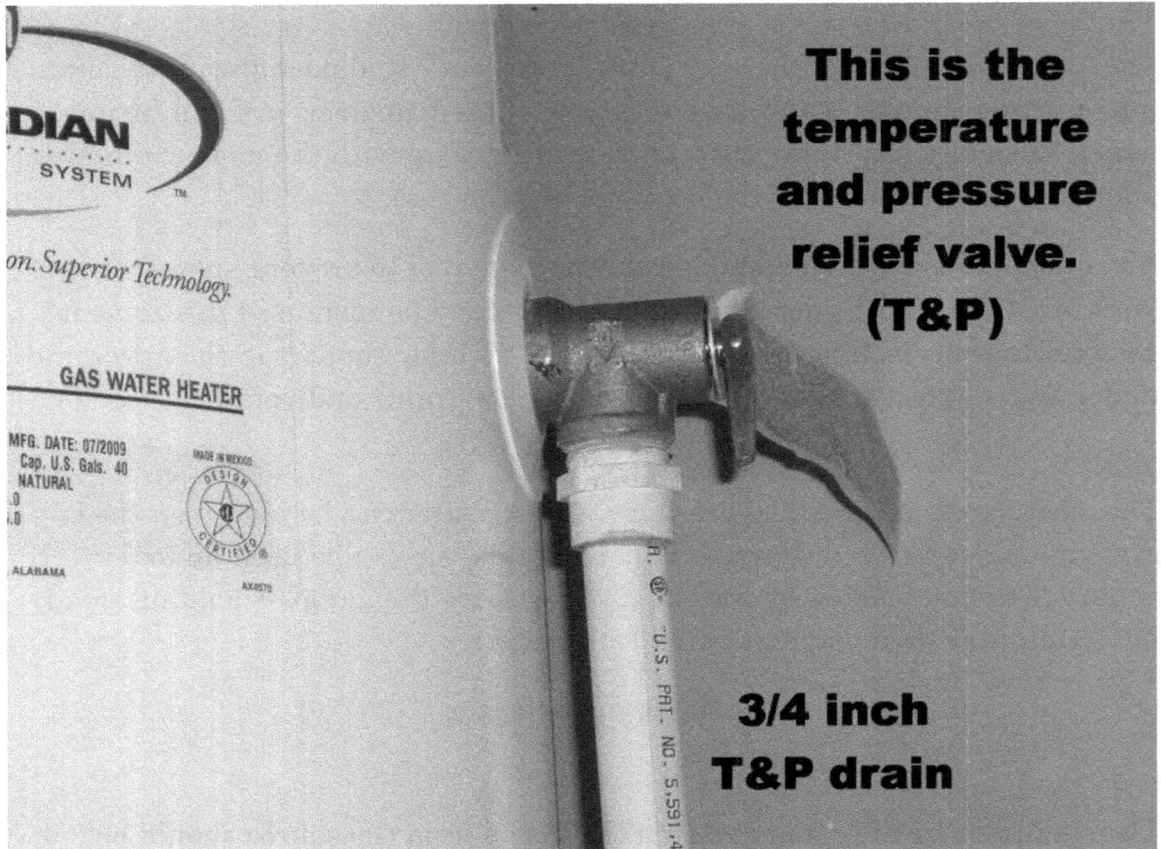

COPPER

Copper lines should be installed neatly and in line with framing members. All joints should be wiped clean as the solder flux is acidic and tends to corrode the pipe. Look at the solder to verify it is of the lead free variety. Solder and flux must not have more than 0.2% lead. Make sure copper piping is not secured with steel or any other material which will propagate electrolysis and cause a leak later. Also, check for nails in the copper pipes. Sometimes it is years before the leak shows up.

CHLORINATED POLYVINYL CHLORIDE (CPVC)

This material has gained a lot of popularity within the industry when copper increased in price. If this material is being used, then ask that both the hot and cold be run in the same material. Some people run the cold in PVC. In my opinion, PVC's tolerances are too close for comfort. CPVC must also be supported every 48 inches. Verify good secure blocking is used when a change to another material is made. The plastic can't handle much torque when a nipple or valve is being replaced.

CROSS-LINKED POLYETHYLENE (PEX)

The PEX installation may not look as neat as the previous two. The material normally comes in rolls and is bent around corners with much fewer fittings installed. It may also come in colors such as red or blue. Many plumbers coordinate the colors to match the hot and cold. This material uses special tools to connect the fittings. The important thing to remember is if it is not connected exactly as the manufacturer specifies, it voids the warranty.

The material expands and contracts with temperature changes more than the other two materials I've discussed. Long runs will need room to move. The lines need to be secured in a way that prevents knocking since this material will move a lot. Shake the piping with your hand to see if it will clunk or rattle.

Check online and download installation manuals for any of the materials being used on your site. If it isn't being installed per the installation guidelines, find out why!

GAS SYSTEM

MATERIALS
The materials used for conducting gas through a house will vary with each plumber. The two most common materials are steel pipe and Corrugated Stainless Steel Tubing (CSST). Stay away from copper piping for gas as some of the additives may corrode the inside of the line. Steel pipe is cut, threaded, and fitted into place on site. A sealant is used on the threads of each pipe at joints. The CSST comes on a roll and fittings are made according to the

manufacturer's installation manual. Different brands have different methods and usually require the plumber to attend the manufacturer's class on installation. Get a manual and read it. CSST will be installed loosely so that nails driven through wall and roofs will not be as likely to pierce the line.

REAMING STEEL PIPES

If you can watch the plumber doing the installation, see that the steel pipes are being reamed to their full size once they have been cut and threaded. The process of cutting will reduce the size of the pipe. I've been on some jobs where the plumber didn't even own a reamer. Note that filing out the burrs with a file is not an acceptable alternative.

SIZING

Sizing the pipe is important and gets into a lot of math, so I will stick to the basics. If you want to do the math a good resource is Code Check - www.codecheck.com/cc/index.html.

First there are two basic designs, a low pressure system and a high pressure system. The low pressure system will have the pressure for the whole house regulated at the meter or before the gas enters the house. In this case the size of the pipe is large to accommodate the quantity of gas needed. Look for a pipe of 1 1/2 inch outside diameter or larger from the outside into the first time it branches off. This is for three or four normal size appliances.

A high pressure system will not need as large a pipe due to the higher pressure. Now you look for a regulator in the house, attic or crawl space. There may be one regulator or one for each appliance. Regulators are spring loaded devices which prevent too much pressure from damaging an appliance. In this case, the same size piping material may be run throughout the entire house.

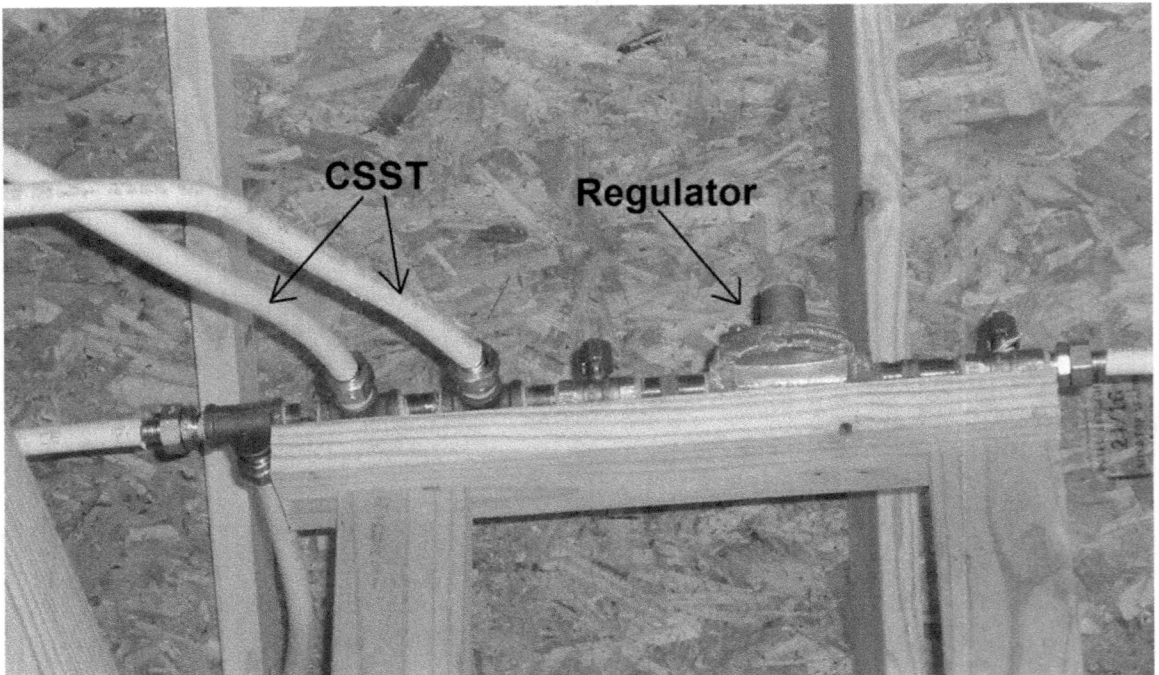

UNDERGROUND

If any of the gas is installed underground it will likely be installed in plastic. Never allow it to be installed under the poured on grade concrete floor. Very stringent rules apply here and I recommend not doing it at all. If steel pipes are installed underground then verify they are "factory wrapped" with a material which resembles asphalt. Only the joints are wrapped on site and those are wrapped tight to prevent electrolysis or moisture from affecting the steel.

TESTING

Testing a gas system in a home should be done twice; once during the plumbing top-out inspection and once before the plumbing final inspection. This test should use a diaphragm type gauge which shows 1/10 pound increments. On a low pressure system use a gauge with a 15 psi red line. This means the center of the gauge would be about 7 1/2 psi. This is where it should be aired up to. Never air it up in the red line area. This is the area where the gauge will be overloaded and it could damage the gauge.

On a high pressure system, a 30 pound gauge is normally used, and the test is at 15 psi. On each of the areas on the appliance side of the regulator(s) the low pressure test must occur. The authority having jurisdiction may have other standards for these tests.

On both tests the pressure must not move for fifteen minutes.

MECHANICAL
ROUGH-IN

GENERAL

The mechanical system consists of all equipment which moves air or conditions space. This will include:

- Heating
- Cooling
- Exhaust

Verify copper piping used for refrigerant is insulated to prevent sweating in the walls and have no nails or staples shot into the pipe. Make sure they don't come into contact with any nonferrous metals which will cause electrolysis. Look at duct placement to prevent the return vent from being placed in the kitchen, bathroom or garage. If you want to condition your garage, use a separate system than the one for living space.

I believe in balancing the house. I prefer using ducts to cross over from bedrooms to other areas or running return ducts into bedrooms. In this country it appears we are living in our bedrooms more, especially younger people.

HEATING

There are as wide variety of heating systems as there are climates, and there should be. From the basic gas or electric furnace which I am more familiar with, to hydronic floor heating systems which work well where temperatures stay low for long periods of time. They all have a few things in common.

Heating appliances simply get hot. Make sure they have clearances from anything combustible. What is combustible? If it isn't stone or steel, it's combustible. Yes, fire rated sheetrock is combustible.

Any appliance which uses a fuel must have access to combustion air. You don't want the appliance burning up oxygen intended for you to breathe. There are several ways this is accomplished and usually it means bringing air from outside the house or ventilated attic space. Homes this day in age are extremely tight. It is dangerous to burn up oxygen from inside.

COOLING

Air conditioning, if you need it, is usually consolidated in with your heating system. The demon to watch out for is moisture. The process of cooling air removes the moisture from it and forms condensation. The evaporator will collect the condensation in a pan is drained to a safe place of disposal. If you know where this point of disposal is then you've won half the battle.

Common places of disposal are:

- In lavatory drain tail pieces
- In bath tub overflow tubes
- In clothes washer stand pipes
- Outside on the ground

If the 3/4 inch PVC drain is stubbed out by a lavatory, make sure you're not placing a pedestal in the spot. The connection is not pleasant to look at, though it is functional. Never let the drain go to a plumbing vent as they are not protected by traps. (See vents in the plumbing top-out section.) I see no issues in draining a small system on the ground if it is in a place where it will not be a nuisance.

A small vent/clean-out is normally placed on the condensate drain near the air handler. A cup of bleach poured down this clean-out twice a year will help to keep algae from stopping the drain up. An emergency drain pan is placed under these units to catch overflows when the drain does stop up. They would drain out over a window to alert you a problem exists. These emergency drains must extend through the soffit and will be visible outside.

EXHAUSTS AND VENTS

FLUE VENTS

This covers more than you might think. The safety involving the design in exhausting flue and other gasses are paramount. Let's look at the flue first. Normally flue vents from gas fired appliances such as water heaters and furnaces are ducted outside through a duct known as a B-Vent. This type of vent requires a 1 inch air gap around it to prevent heat from the vent from igniting combustible materials.

Look at each exhaust vent which conducts flue gasses to verify what the clearance from combustible materials are. Each section will have the required clearance labeled on the pipe. Some types of flue vents require up to 6 inches of clearance. Where these vents pass through ceilings or walls, sheet metal is used to close up the open space and hold the pipe in the center of the space.

Verify that each section of pipes is supported separately per the manufacturer's installation instructions. If it extends above the roof more than 5 feet, guy wires may need to be used. Don't allow any exhaust to come out below an operable window or within 8 feet of a wall. Watch for caps to be installed on the flue pipe, and make sure the flashing is properly sealed at the roof. If you can see light from below, then this is a red flag.

This metal fire stop will keep the vent in the center of the hole away from combustables.

The fire stop shold be attached to the ceiling. No screws should be in the pipe!

The storm collar not properly installed is another common mistake made. It is due to an oversight of the workman installing a gas appliance. The storm collar prevents rain from running down the flue pipe and into the home. What occurs is this: the roofer will install the flashing, also known as a roof jack, and drop the flue pipe down the hole. The storm collar will slide up the pipe while the pipe hangs inside the house. When the plumber installs the water heater, he lifts up the flue and connects it to the draft hood of the appliance which leaves the storm collar pushed up high above the flashing. This is the way it is sometimes left. The storm collar should be just above the roof jack. Additionally, it should be sealed to the pipe with a high heat sealant.

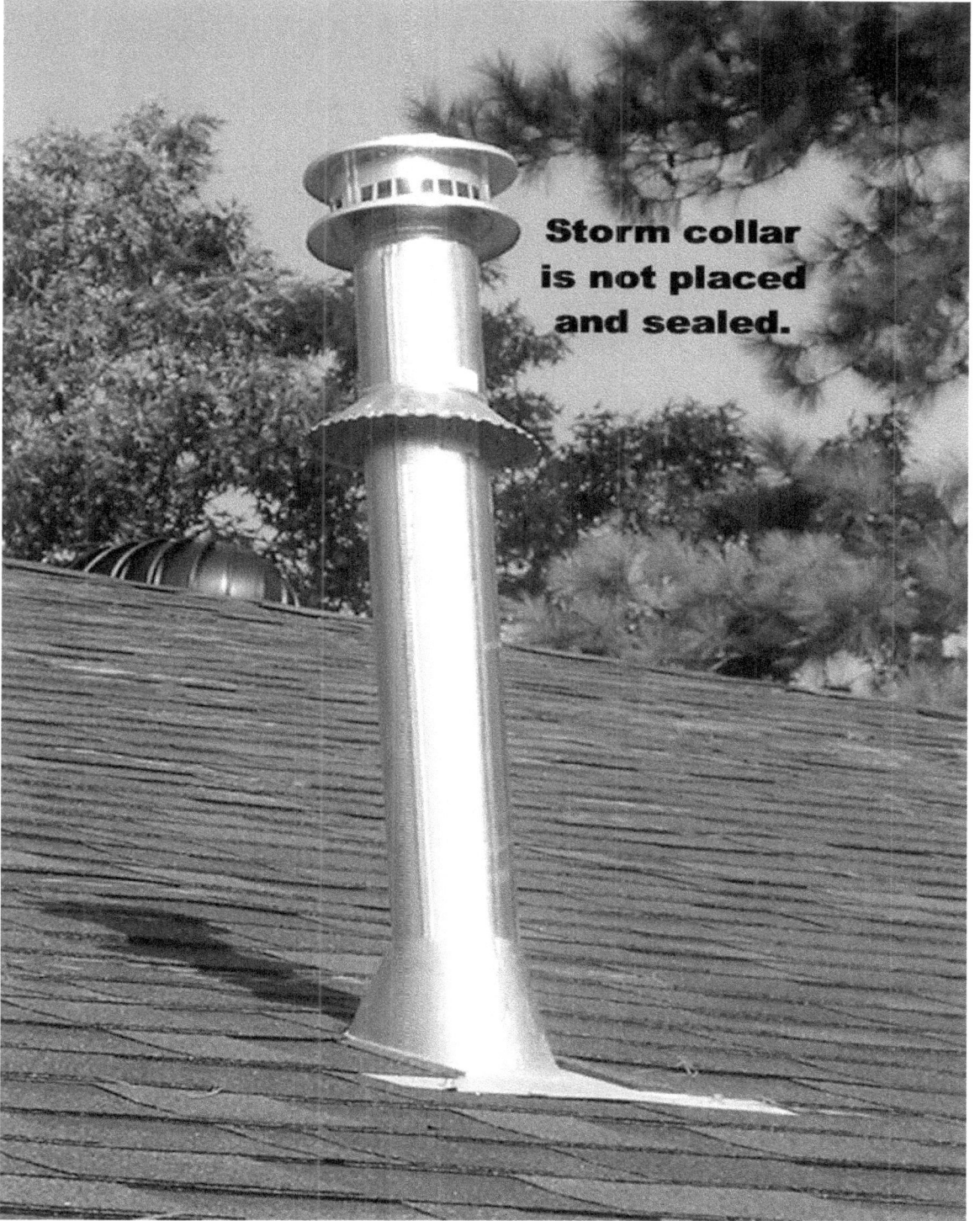

Storm collar
is not placed
and sealed.

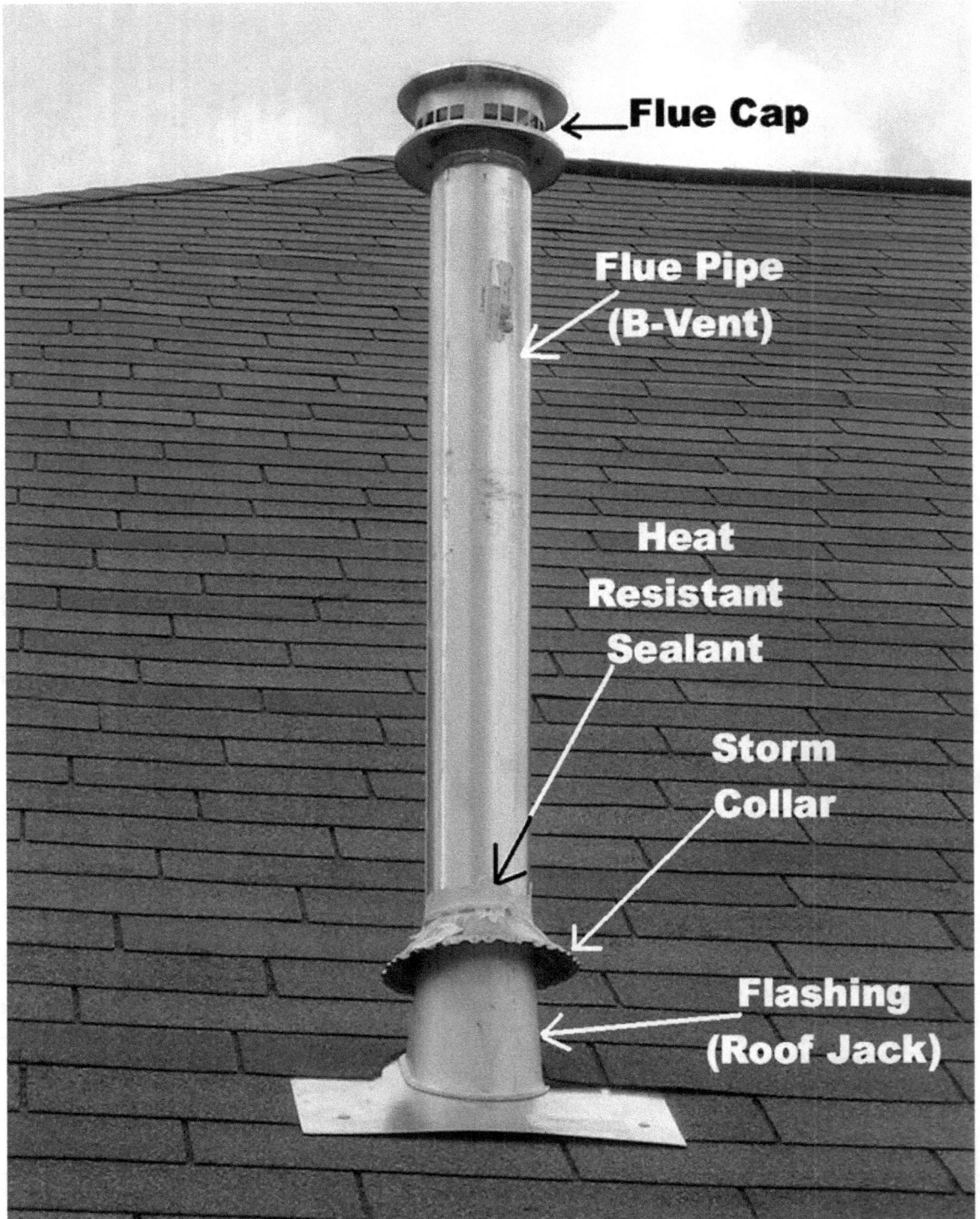

Flue Cap

Flue Pipe (B-Vent)

Heat Resistant Sealant

Storm Collar

Flashing (Roof Jack)

64

DRYER

Dryer exhaust ducts must be smooth wall steel with joints placed in the direction of airflow. Never allow screws or other fasteners to be used that may catch lint inside the duct. If possible, the dryer should be placed on an exterior wall to keep this vent as short as possible. It should terminate outside the house in a metal cover with a back draft damper (A metal flapper to prevent other things from entering). A dryer exhaust must **never** have a screen on it.

FIREPLACE

Wood burning fireplaces need to be ducted out through the roof and be high enough to prevent catching the roof on fire. The bottom of the fireplace flue cap must be 2 feet higher than any portion of the house within 10 feet horizontally from the cap.

SMALL EXHAUST

Bathroom exhaust fans should be ducted outside the structure. Some of these fans are very inexpensively built and don't have a lot of power. The ducts should be kept short. Exhaust fans are placed in bathing rooms and laundry rooms to remove steam, as well as toilet rooms to remove noxious fumes.

VENT HOOD

When a ducted vent hood is used over a residential stove, the duct should be of a smooth walled metal duct which terminates outside the house. They are required to be ducted out if an open broiler is used. If a down draft exhaust for the Jenn-Air range or similar appliance is used, verify the listed cap is used per the manufacturer's installation guide.

DRY WALL AND
FIRE PROTECTION

We have touched on a small part of fire blocking in our discussion of framing. Fire blocking is like insurance. When you need it, it's too late to get it.

GARAGE

The next step is to address the garage. Many fires start there and you don't want a fire to come in the house while you're sleeping. Any door from the house into the attached garage must be a solid wood or steel door without windows. A window will let a fire through in an instant. Never put a door into the garage from a room where a person will sleep!

The ceiling and walls between the garage and the house or attic should have 5/8 inch type X sheetrock. This material has fibers built into it to help prevent nails from letting go in the high temperatures imposed during a fire.

If an attic access is in the garage, then pay a little extra for a fire rated drop down ladder. If a stairway is in the garage going up to the attic, it should have the same type door as discussed earlier. The garage should never have a door into a sleeping room.

I would like to see smoke detectors placed in garages which are electrically interconnected to the others in the house. Setting off every detector in the house would surely wake everyone up if an automobile was on fire. Building Codes do not require this at this time.

SMOKE DETECTORS

Smoke detectors must be placed in every sleeping room and in the hall or foyer outside the sleeping rooms. I say sleeping room, because many people have rooms which are not bedrooms, but they are used as guest sleeping areas. We need to protect these guests as well. Each floor of the house must have at least one smoke detector installed.

Smoke detectors must operate off the home's electrical system and have a battery backup. They must also be electrically connected, which means they will have a separate wire running from one to the next which is used to signal all the detectors when one is activated. When one goes off, they all should go off.

Smoke detectors should be kept more than 6 inches from any corner made by a ceiling and a wall. Smoke doesn't go there. They should also be kept at least 3 feet away from heating & air conditioning supply grills. However, locations near the return are okay.

UTILITY ROOMS

Appliance closets or other utility rooms where equipment may be placed must have a ceiling installed. If combustion air is needed in the closet, then it must be brought through the ceiling or wall in steel ducts. These ceilings are there to slow fire down, so have your contractor seal it tightly.

FIRE PLACES

Make sure the fireplace has a defined hearth. Many contractors placing tile in the family room assume that, since tile is none combustible then no hearth is needed. The defining of the hearth area gives people a line not to cross. Don't stack Christmas gifts there... Also, when the future owner of the house has a real estate inspector look over the house, this won't be another code violation. The same tile used on the floor can be rotated one eighth of a turn to define the hearth area. It's clean, attractive and won't normally cost any extra.

ELECTRICAL

SERVICES

Get the power on! The cabinets are in, the power is on and you can plug the radio in. Let's take a look around. Starting at the source, we look at what is called the "electrical service"; this includes the meter and the breaker panel. If the meter and the breaker panel are not close to each other or on opposite sides of a wall, then a breaker or large fused switch will be by the meter. Look around to verify a ground rod with a cable about the size of a pencil or lager is connected to it. This is your supplemental ground. We looked at the main one on the electrical rough-in section.

Have the electrician remove the breaker panel cover and look at the wires in the box. Don't stick your hand in there, it is hot! Just look at the wires and whether or not they reflect the workmanship of a person who takes pride in their work. If they are crammed in the box with no rhyme or reason, then a talk with the master electrician may be required.

ATTIC

Next, check the attic and crawl spaces to look for any cable crossing catwalks where damage could occur when accessing the walkway. They should be protected from damage. Placing a board next to the cable is an acceptable method to protect those exposed on catwalks. A switch for the light should be at the access point to the attic or any crawl space where equipment is located.

KITCHEN

The kitchen counter top receptacles must be Ground Fault Circuit Interrupter (GFCI) protected. This is for your safety and should be tested to see if they work. Go to your home improvement center and purchase a tester for GFCI receptacles. The testers range in cost from $7 to $15 dollars. When you plug in the tester, the three lights tell you if the plug is wired correctly. When you push the button, it should trip the GFCI switch. Make sure the receptacles reset.

BATHROOM
Check the receptacles in the bathroom as well. ALL receptacles in a bathroom or toilet room must be GFCI protected.

BEDROOMS
Bedroom receptacles must be Arc-Fault protected. In fact the 2009 electrical code requires all 15 and 20 amp circuits which are not GFCI protected must be Arc-Fault protected. I have mixed feelings on this, but in my business, it's better to err on the side of safety. In any case, do not mix GFCI and Arc-Fault protected circuits; they just don't work well together.

GARAGE
Garage receptacles are required to be GFCI protected unless you have a dedicated appliance plug such as a freezer.

OTHER
All receptacles outside the home (other than for deicing) or around pools and spas must be GFCI protected.

Plug covers should be tight with no gaps. If the plugs move when you test them, then the plugs may not be properly installed. Remove a cover from a switch. The box should be within 1/16 inch from the face of the sheet rock. The hole the box is in should be no more than 1/8 inch larger than the box itself.

Make sure light switches are installed at the top and bottom of stairs.

Light fixtures in clothes closets must not have open bulbs or pull chains.

No electrical switch or receptacle should be within 3 feet of the bathtub or shower, and 5 feet from a spa or pool.

PLUMBING

KITCHEN
Put the plugs in the drains and fill all sinks to within an inch of the top. Look under the cabinets for leaks. Pull the plugs, turn on the disposal and watch for leaks again. As the sinks empty, turn the disposal off and listen to the drain as the sink empties. If you hear the P-trap flush like a toilet, then the vent is not breaking its siphon. Look at the ice maker box and verify the trim is on with no open gaps around it.

BATHROOM
Check the lavatory in the same method you checked the kitchen sink. Pull the tank lid off the toilet and flush it. Watch for spewing or loose tubing in the tank. Verify the tank fills to the line the manufacturer has marked inside. Also, verify the valve in the tank is at least one inch above the overflow tube. Look at the bathtub spigot; it should be at least an inch higher than the place the water would be before it overflows. These items may seem small, but they are life saving issues.

LAUNDRY
Make sure the trim is on the washer box with no gaps around it. If a sink is in the laundry, verify it has no leaks just as you did the kitchen and bathroom.

OUTSIDE
On the roof, your plumbing vents should be tall enough to clear any snow build up. All hose connections should be protected by a vacuum breaker, and any irrigation system must have a backflow prevention assembly to protect you. It must be tested upon installation and annually thereafter. There should be a valve on the water line serving the home. This will be the valve you close in case of emergency.

WATER HEATER
On tank type water heaters, verify the Temperature and Pressure (T&P) relief valve is installed in the top 6 inches of the tank. See that the drain from the T&P valve is 3/4 inch and terminates in a safe place.

If the jurisdiction having authority requires a check valve of any kind or a backflow prevention assembly on your water service, verify a device is installed to handle thermal expansion. As water is heated, it expands and will usually back up through the water meter into the city lines. If this point of relief is checked by one of the devices I've just described, then an explosion may occur or other damage. This will usually apply to a water well since wells normally have a check valve in the system which only allows water to travel in one direction.

WATER SOFTENER

Most of the softeners I've encountered have a drain of some type which goes to the sewer system or runs out on the ground. Verify a drain from one of these appliances has an air gap securely built in the system. An air gap is a point where the water drains through the open air to the fixture or pipe leading to the trap. You should be able to pass your hand between the two. This prevents contamination of your drinking water.

MECHANICAL

OUTSIDE

Starting with central air conditioning, the unit outside is referred to as the condenser. It should have a method of turning the power off to the unit within site. The electrical conduit must either be metal conduit, rigid plastic conduit or a flexible watertight conduit. The condenser should be sitting on a concrete or masonry pad.

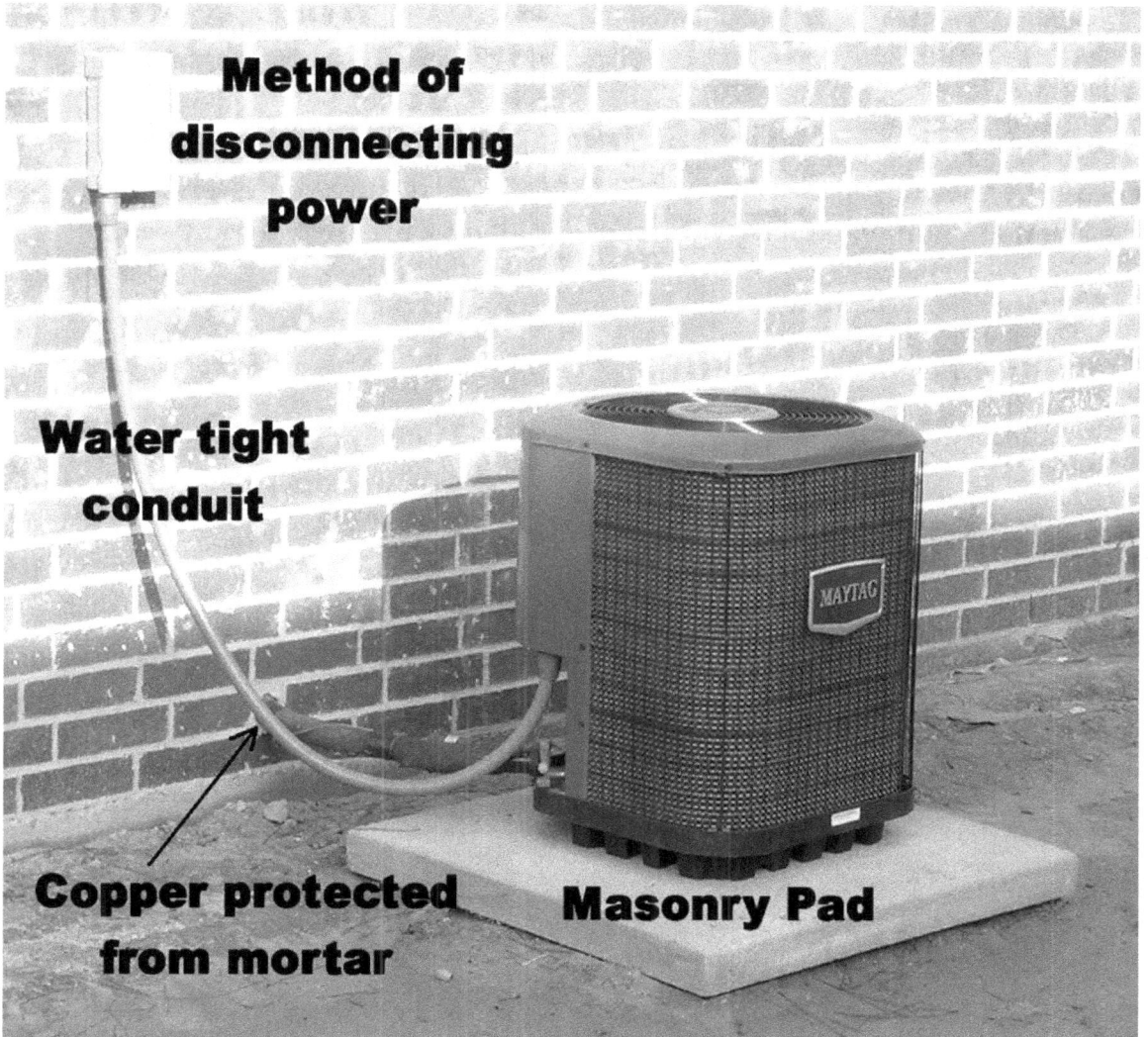

Look at all vent terminations outside. The dryer should not have a screen on it. The Gen-Air down draft stove exhaust should have its cap securely in place. All flues and chimneys must have caps on.

INSIDE

Verify all of the vents have their louvers or grills and work properly. There should be a filter in the return. In mechanical closets, attics or crawl spaces, verify the gas fired furnaces and other heating appliances have combustion air as we discussed earlier. Make sure any doors into the places where gas fired appliances are located have tight weather stripping and self-closers on them. Look at the flexible gas connector. It should not enter the appliance housing or pass through a wall.

Verify the thermostat is in place and is level. Make sure you receive all the installation manuals and service manuals along with any warranty cards.

BUILDING

ADDRESS

You wouldn't think such a small thing would be as important as this is, but your address can mean the difference between life and death. That "magic hour" which is so important for first responders can be whittled down considerably when they can't find you. Get the address out there where it can be seen from the street!

SLOPE

The yard should slope away from the house to prevent water from eroding the area around your foundation. The grade around your house will slowly increase in elevation over the natural course of time. This build up, over a period of several years can eventually cause several other problems. Look for at least 6 inches of fall from the floor height within 10 feet of the house. On pier and beam homes, verify the natural drainage will not cut a path under the house and no water can stand under it.

EGRESS

All exterior doors must have a landing, per code. The landing for your primary path of egress should be no more than 1 1/2 inches lower than the top of the door's threshold.

Stairways must have a hand rail the entire distance of travel. If I am carrying one of my grandsons down the stairs, I want to hold on until I am on a floor!

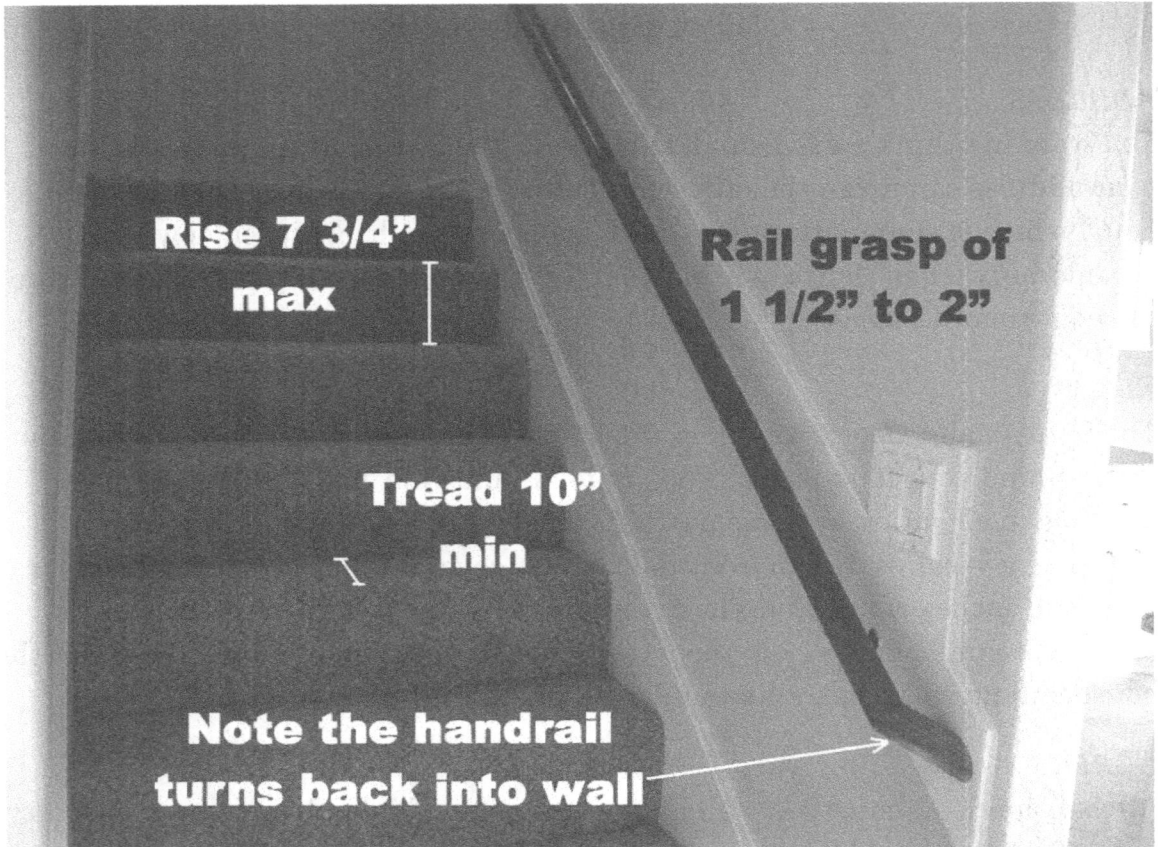

Rise 7 3/4" max

Rail grasp of 1 1/2" to 2"

Tread 10" min

Note the handrail turns back into wall

All sleeping rooms must have a path for emergency egress. Check to see the window opens. Windows used for emergency egress should have openings of at least 5 square feet on the first floor and 5.7 square feet above the first floor. For your fire rescue to access with oxygen on, the openings should also be at least 24 inches high and 20 inches wide.

HAZARDOUS LOCATIONS

The windows within 2 feet of an exterior door, the window over a bath tub or glass around the shower, and windows on stairway landings are all locations one can fall through. These windows should be of tempered glass. Look in the corners of each piece of glass and find the etched marking which is required on tempered glass.

Large picture windows (9 sq. ft & larger) and glass doors are notorious hazards. They too must be tempered in most cases.

Balconies and walkways which are more than 30 inches above grade should have guards to prevent small children from falling through them. There should be no opening large enough to fit a ball 4 inches in diameter through.

ENERGY
CONSERVATION

As people become more educated, they tend to realize the benefits of conserving energy. As the economy fluctuates, it teaches us efficiency has rewards beyond the obvious. The International Energy Conservation Code is a model code designed to create an efficient environment using common materials and building practices.

The important thing to remember is different systems work together to produce the efficiency desired. Address your efficiency needs and wants, make a plan, and stick to your plan. When only a portion of a plan is followed, the home suffers as a whole.

Example: I increase the efficiency of my heating and cooling system but the window upgrades will cost another $1000. If I opt to use the less efficient windows, I may lose the savings on the environmental systems out my windows. I am counting on those savings to pay for themselves by saving utility money. So consider that spending the $1000 extra insures the several thousand spent on environmental equipment will earn a return plus the extra grand.

I look at it this way. If I spend the extra up front of what would be $15 a month on my house note and it saves me an overall $100 monthly on my utility bill, then that is quite a return. Here's the math: add the entire amount extra on each energy savings item. (Tankless water heater - $1200 vs. tank type water heater $850 is a difference of $350) Divide the amount by the number of months of your house note (30 year = 360 months) $350 / 360 = $1.02 per month. Now look at the big yellow tag on the appliances and see how much money is going into your pocket rather than the utility company's pocket. Next, check with your tax preparer and see if the government will pay for one of those appliances!

ENERGYGUIDE

Water Heater - Natural
Capacity (first hour rating):
258 gallons per hour

Rinnai Corporation
Model R94-LSe
R94-LSi

Estimated Yearly Operating Cost

$223

$199 $290

Cost Range of Similar Models

183 therms

Estimated Yearly Energy Use

Your cost will depend on your utility rates and use.

- Cost range based only on models of similar capacity fueled by natural gas.
- Estimated operating cost based on a 2007 national average natural gas cost of $1.218 per therm
- For more information, visit www.ftc.gov/appliances.

(VA2535-N)
U287-560-1X01

172 00012 56047 9

energy
ENERGY STAR

REScheck

The REScheck is an engineering program offered for free by the U.S. Department of Energy to help you design and build in an efficient method. The program should be run during the design process and definitely before you build. You may well decide to change some things. Go to www.energycodes.gov/rescheck/download.stm to obtain your copy.

NFRC

The National Fenestration Rating Council (NFRC) provides accurate information to measure and compare energy performance for windows, doors and skylights. The important numbers on the labels are Solar Heat Gain Coefficient (SHGC) and the U-Factor. I won't address what all of this means, but the required values are on the REScheck (above) and to obtain the efficiency you desire, these values should be checked BEFORE the windows are installed or even purchased.

Watch for counterfeit labels. The certification seal in the corner of the label must be present. Windows built on site will not have these labels and are issued a default value for your REScheck to use. The International Energy Conservation Code has tables to help with this.

Left label:

NFRC CERTIFIED

ADW
S-300 SH WINDOW
ALUMINUM FRAME
COL 270 LOW-E GLASS
3/8" Spacer

ENERGY PERFORMANCE RATINGS

| 0.51 | 0.30 |

ADDITIONAL PERFORMANCE RATINGS

| 0.55 | — |

MFR PLANT ID 1

Right label:

Builders FirstSource   800-981-6773   www.buildersfirstsource.com

National Fenestration Rating Council® CERTIFIED

SERIES 9810 Single Hung
Vinyl Frame Doulbe Glaze
Low E Glass with Internal Muntins

ENERGY PERFORMANCE RATINGS

U-Factor (U.S./I-P)	Solar Heat Gain Coefficient
0.36	0.27

ADDITIONAL PERFORMANCE RATINGS

Visible Transmittance	
0.49	—

Manufacturer stipulates that these ratings conform to applicable NFRC procedures for determining whole product performance. NFRC ratings are determined for a fixed set of environmental conditions and a specific product size. NFRC does not recommend any product and does not warrant the suitability of any product for any specific use. Consult manufacturers literature for other product performance information.
www.nfrc.org

INSULATION

The insulation values you want to use will be displayed on the REScheck you have acquired. Verify the proper value is installed by the R-Value which must be printed on the insulation every 6 feet. If the insulation is of the blown type or expanding foam, the insulation installer must produce a certification showing the type, quantity and R-Value for the building element insulated.

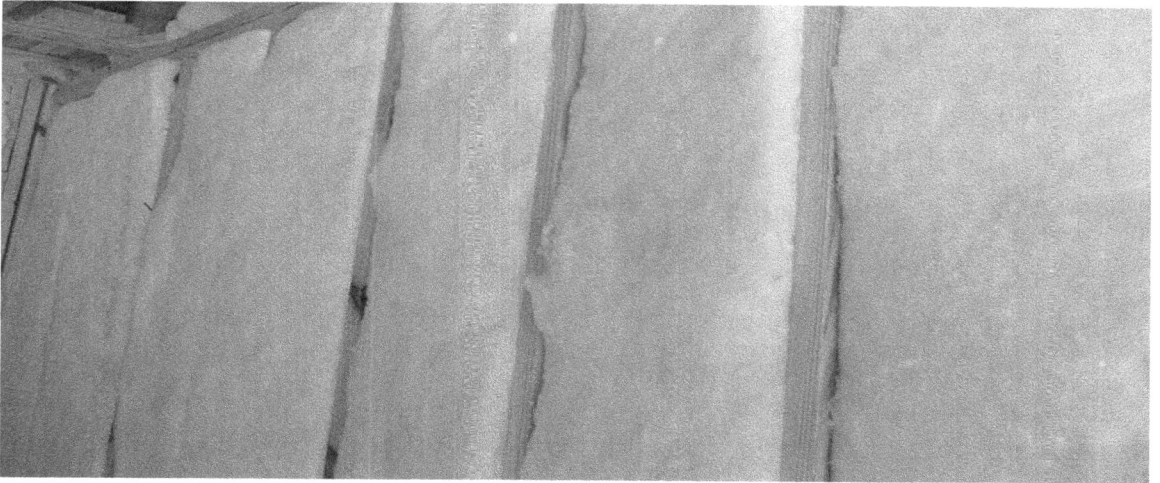

Verify the batts or blown insulation is not compacted. Compacted insulation has an R-Value of zero. Verify all openings into areas where the air isn't conditioned or heated are sealed. This would include holes bored through top and bottom wall plates, floors cut out under bathtubs, around window and door framing and around any penetration in the inside or outside walls. Check to see showers and tubs on exterior walls have insulation behind them before they are installed. It is not uncommon for interior walls or floors to be insulated to reduce sound transmission.

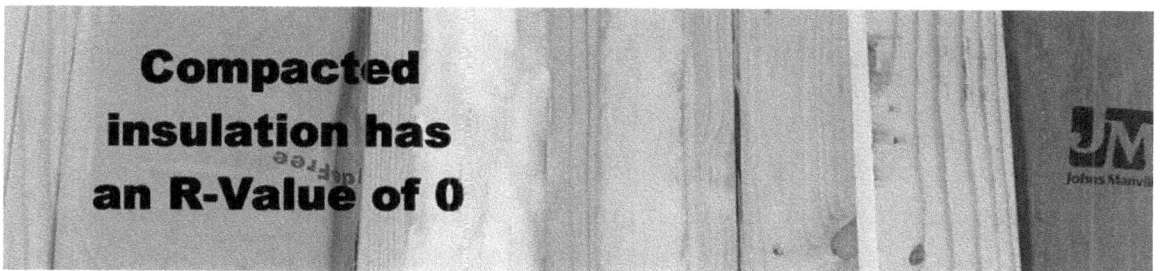

Compacted insulation has an R-Value of 0

APPLIANCE EFFICIENCIES

Some very efficient appliances are on the market these days. Shop around and do your research on what to buy. Specify to your contractor which efficiencies you want regarding mechanical equipment. This is usually more important than brand names. There are only four or five domestic manufacturers producing equipment for mechanical systems.

GAS

Most companies can supply you with furnaces, water heaters and boilers which have 98% efficiency. This means 98% of the heat produced by burning the fuel is actually used. Most of the systems in use today are only 80% efficient. That's like losing 1/5 of your gas into the atmosphere.

AIR CONDITIONING

A/C efficiency is measured by a Seasonal Energy Efficiency Ratio (SEER) rating. Simply stated, this is the input of energy divided by the output energy in a typical seasonal day. The average home uses a 13 SEER system. My home has an 18 SEER system and I can tell from my low power bill. They make even higher efficiencies now. The extra cost up front is positively worth it in warmer climates.

If you are located in a high humidity climate, a humidistat is a must. By keeping the humidity between 45% and 50% the comfort level increases dramatically without bringing the temperature down. Also molds grow better in humidity's above 55% and below 45%.

Ceiling fans make a difference whether you're heating or cooling. A programmable thermostat makes a difference as well. Get the paperwork for all this equipment and read through it. Knowing how to program your system to meet your unique needs can save you a lot of money.

The duct system also has insulation values you should watch for. These values are preset in the REScheck program and are often not followed. Look for the value on the duct itself or where applicable on the insulation wrapped around the duct. Check to see all of the duct joints are sealed up tight and is installed as the installation instructions direct.

ETL
LISTED
US
90131
G059077080
AIR DUCT CLASS 1

ade
Thermal Performance

MAXIMUM VELOCITY
MAXIMUM POSITIVE PRESSURE
MAXIMUM NEGATIVE PRESSURE

6000 fpm
10 IN W.C.
1/2IN W.C.

FLAME SPREAD - 25 SMOKE DEVELOPMENT - 50
R - 8.0 ASTM C-518
CONFORMS TO UL STD 181
QUIETFLEX MFG. CO. L.P., HOUSTON, TEXAS

7

WATER HEATERS

The tank type water heater has been very dependable over the years and efficiency is the only thing I have against a properly installed one. The tankless water heaters have proven very efficient and they have been in use for decades in Europe. Both electric and gas are available although gas seems to be the most efficient. Some models installs inside the wall which prevents using valuable floor space for equipment closets or unattractive appliances in the garage. The advantage to this technology is the water is not heated until it is needed, whereas a tank type will keep the water hot and in storage waiting for use.

The method of sizing seems to raise a lot of questions for plumbers who do not use this technology on a daily basis. First you must know the average temperature of the water when it enters the home. Second, you need to know how many gallons of water per minute you will use at one time. A table in the plumbing section of the International Residential Code gives default values for peak demand for fixtures. Assuming only one fixture will be used in a restroom at a time, here are the fixture values in gallons per minute which use the most HOT water:

- Shower – 1 gpm
- Kitchen sink – 1 gpm
- Dishwasher – 1.4 gpm
- Clothes Washer – 1 gpm

With this information, read the manufacturer's instruction sheets and verify that you size the water heater to match this or better. The tankless water heater will only heat what you need, but if you have family over for the holidays, you may exceed its capacity if it isn't properly sized.

Gas fired tankless water heater

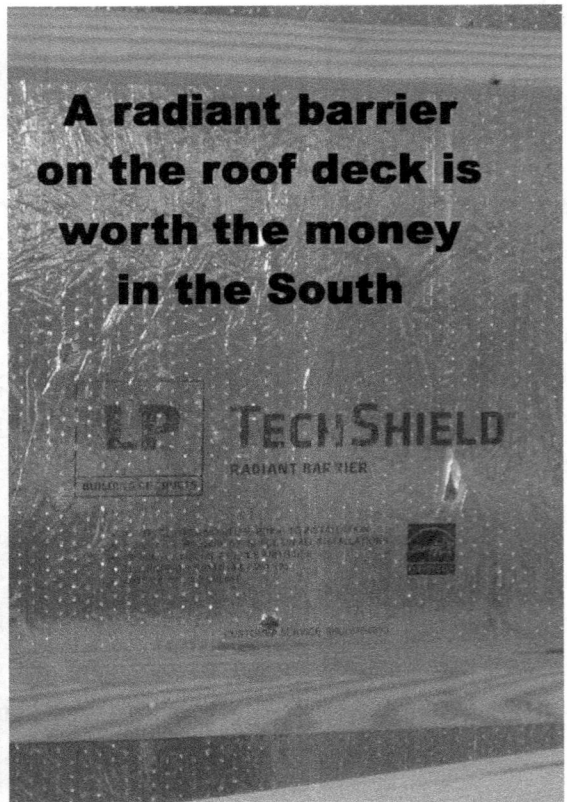

A radiant barrier on the roof deck is worth the money in the South

Concluding Comment

If only one mistake I've covered in this book was prevented, you've paid for the book. Preventing mistakes and oversights could save your life, so take the time to protect your life and your investment. Good luck with your new construction project.

Take your time, do your homework, read the manufacturers installation instructions. Remember the inspector is out there for your safety!

RESOURCES AVAILABLE FOR YOUR BENEFIT

Acme Brick - www.brick.com

American National Standards Institute (ANSI) - www.ansi.org

American Society of Heating, Refrigerating and Air-Conditioning Engineers (ASHRAE) - www.ashrae.org

American Society of Sanitary Engineering - www.asse-plumbing.org

Association of the Wall and Ceiling Industry (AWCI) – www.store.awci.org

American Wood Council (AWC) - www.awc.org

Building Envelope Design Guide – Glazing - www.wbdg.org/design/env_fenestration_glz.php

Canadian Standards Association (CSA) - www.csa.ca/cm/home

CertainTeed Building Products - www.certainteed.com

Code Check - www.codecheck.com/cc/index.html

Concrete Reinforcing Steel Institute (CRSI) - www.crsi.org

Dow Building Solutions – www.building.dow.com

Hardie Panel Siding - www.jameshardie.com/homeowner

Information and videos - www.buildingscience.com

International Code Council – www.iccsafe.org

Jenn-Air - www.jennair.com

National Fire Protection Association (NFPA) - www.nfpa.org

Owens Corning - www.owenscorning.com

OSB Guide – www.osbguide.tecotested.com

Rinnai - www.rinnai.us

Southern Pine Bureau (SPIB) - www.spib.org

TechShield - www.lpcorp.com/radiantbarrier/radiantbarrier.aspx

The Engineered Wood Association - www.apawood.org

Tyvek Manufacturer - www2.dupont.com

Underwriters Laboratories (UL) - www.ul.com/global/eng/pages

Uniform Codes - www.iapmo.org

US Department of Energy - www.energycodes.gov/rescheck/download.stm

www.ingramcontent.com/pod-product-compliance
Lightning Source LLC
Chambersburg PA
CBHW081659270326
41933CB00017B/3216